Max
on Life

INSPIRATIONAL

On the Anvil (1985)

No Wonder They Call Him the Savior
(1986)

God Came Near (1987)

Six Hours One Friday (1989)

The Applause of Heaven (1990)

In the Eye of the Storm (1991)

And the Angels Were Silent (1992)

He Still Moves Stones (1993)

When God Whispers Your Name (1994)

A Gentle Thunder (1995)

In the Grip of Grace (1996)

The Great House of God (1997)

Just Like Jesus (1998)

When Christ Comes (1999)

He Chose the Nails (2000)

Traveling Light (2001)

A Love Worth Giving (2002)

Next Door Savior (2003)

Come Thirsty (2004)

It's Not About Me (2004)

Cure for the Common Life (2005)

Facing Your Giants (2006)

3:16 (2007)

Every Day Deserves a Chance (2007)

Cast of Characters (2008)

Fearless (2009)

Outlive Your Life (2010)

FICTION

An Angel's Story

The Christmas Candle

The Christmas Child

GIFT BOOKS

A Heart Like Jesus

Everyday Blessings

For These Tough Times

God's Mirror

God's Promises for You

God Thinks You're Wonderful

Grace for the Moment, Vols. I & II

Grace for the Moment Journal

In the Beginning

Just for You

Just Like Jesus Devotional

Let the Journey Begin

Max on Life series

Mocha with Max

One Incredible Moment

Safe in the Shepherd's Arms

The Cross

The Gift for All People

The Greatest Moments

Traveling Light for Mothers

Traveling Light Journal

Turn

Walking with the Savior

You: God's Brand-New Idea!

BIBLES (GENERAL EDITOR)

Grace for the Moment Daily Bible

He Did This Just for You (New Testament)

The Devotional Bible

The Lucado Life Lessons Study Bible

Max on Life

Answers and Insights to Your
Most Important Questions

MAX LUCADO

THOMAS NELSON
Since 1798

NASHVILLE   DALLAS   MEXICO CITY   RIO DE JANEIRO

Published in Nashville, Tennessee, by Thomas Nelson. Thomas Nelson is a registered trademark of Thomas Nelson, Inc.

Thomas Nelson, Inc., titles may be purchased in bulk for educational, business, fund-raising, or sales promotional use. For information, please e-mail SpecialMarkets@ThomasNelson.com.

Unless otherwise noted, Scripture quotations are taken from The Holy Bible, New International Version®, NIV®. Copyright © 1973, 1978, 1984 by Biblica, Inc.™ Used by permission of Zondervan. All rights reserved worldwide. www.zondervan.com.

Other Scripture references are from the following sources: The Amplified Bible (AMPLIFIED BIBLE): Old Testament. © 1962, 1964 by Zondervan (used by permission); and from The Amplified Bible: New Testament. © 1958 by the Lockman Foundation (used by permission). The Contemporary English Version (CEV). © 1991 by the American Bible Society. Used by permission. The English Standard Version (ESV). © 2001 by Crossway Bibles, a division of Good News Publishers. God's Word (GOD'S WORD) is a copyrighted work of God's Word to the Nations Bible Society. Quotations are used by permission. © 1995 by God's Word to the Nations Bible Society. All rights reserved. The Jerusalem Bible (JERUSALEM BIBLE). © 1966 by Darton, Longman & Todd Ltd. and Doubleday & Company, Inc. Used by permission. The King James Version (KJV). The Message (MSG) by Eugene H. Peterson. © 1993, 1994, 1995, 1996, 2000. Used by permission of NavPress Publishing Group. All rights reserved. The New American Standard Bible® (NASB). © The Lockman Foundation 1960, 1962, 1963, 1968, 1971, 1972, 1973, 1975, 1977, 1995. Used by permission. The New Century Version® (NCV). © 2005 by Thomas Nelson, Inc. Used by permission. All rights reserved. The New English Bible (NEB). © 1961, 1970 by The Delegates of the Oxford University Press and the Syndics of the Cambridge University Press. Reprinted by permission. The New King James Version® (NKJV). © 1982 by Thomas Nelson, Inc. Used by permission. All rights reserved. The Holy Bible, New Living Translation (NLT). © 1996, 2004. Used by permission of Tyndale House Publishers, Inc., Wheaton, Illinois 60189. All rights reserved. The New Scofield Bible (NEW SCOFIELD BIBLE). © 1967 by Oxford University Press, Inc. J. B. Phillips: The New Testament in Modern English, Revised Edition (PHILLIPS). © J. B. Phillips 1958, 1960, 1972. Used by permission of Macmillan Publishing Co., Inc. Revised Standard Version of the Bible (RSV). © 1946, 1952, 1971, 1973 by the Division of Christian Education of the National Council of the Churches of Christ in the U.S.A. Used by permission. Today's English Version (TEV). © American Bible Society 1966, 1971, 1976, 1992. The Living Bible (TLB). © 1971. Used by permission of Tyndale House Publishers, Inc., Wheaton, Illinois 60189. All rights reserved. The Weymouth New Testament (WEYMOUTH).

ISBN 978-0-8499-4874-9 (IE)

Library of Congress Cataloging-in-Publication Data

Lucado, Max.
    Max on life : answers and inspiration for life's questions / Max Lucado.
        p. cm.
    Includes bibliographical references (p. 237–8) and indexes.
    ISBN 978-0-8499-4812-1 (hardcover)
    1. Christian life—Miscellanea. 2. Theology, Doctrinal—Popular works. I. Title.
    BV4501.3.L8461 2011
    230'.04624—dc22   2010040268

Printed in the United States of America

11 12 13 14 15 RRD 6 5 4 3 2 1

To David and Cathy Moberg

For more than two decades you have kept a
steady hand on this publishing vessel.

Thanks for countless prayers, encouragement,
and ideas (of which this book is one).

Contents

Acknowledgments

My longtime editorial assistant, Karen Hill, really carried the load on this effort. Thank you, Karen, for sorting through stacks of letters, sermons, and e-mails. You deserve a long vacation.

So do you, Carol Bartley. You are to manuscripts what a car wash is to an automobile. Thanks to your polish and buffing: this manuscript reads better than I wrote it.

Paula Major, I especially appreciate your willingness to tackle such a mammoth project. Great work!

Troy Schmidt, thank you for the tag-team effort. The task was much easier because of you!

Terry Gibbs, you are a vault of wisdom and a source of inspiration. I give you loud applause!

Ambassador Advertising folks, thanks for the spadework in making audio messages available.

Steve and Cheryl Green, Greg and Susan Ligon, Dave Schroeder, and the rest of the team, my hat is off to you.

A special word for the UpWords team: Tina Chisholm, Margaret Mechinus, and Jennifer Bowman. You receive each call with kindness and respond to each inquiry with grace.

Since 1988, the Oak Hills Church has provided me a greenhouse for ideas. Many of these questions were first asked by this wonderful flock. Thanks for taking the time to think.

And Denalyn, my wife, the one question I cannot answer is, how could a mule like me marry a princess like you? Oh the wonder of fairy tales.

Before We Begin . . .

We have questions. Real, important, and challenging questions. You have yours. I have mine. We pepper our questions with *whys*, *whens*, *whats*, and *how comes*.

We've created a question mark to highlight our questions. It's stooped and bent, perhaps because questions can leave us in the same shape, burdened and weary. We have deep, heavy questions.

We crave answers. Straighten this mark, and let it stand. Replace the cowering curl with a confident exclamation point.

Easier said than done.

Some questions defy easy answers. But you know that. You've been looking. I know that. I've been looking as well.

Through the years I've received lots of letters. Some are profound, some are heartbreaking. Some even make me smile—like this note from one of our church members, my good buddy Sammy. He was seven years old.

> Dear Max,
>
> I'm sorry for pulling the fire alarm after 11:30 service. Please forgive me. My parents have punished me but I want to make it right with you. Please let me know what I can do.
>
> in Christ's love
> Sammy

Pastors receive many letters. Writers are asked many questions. Being both a pastor and a writer, I've heard more than my share. And they've shaped my thoughts. Genuine questions have determined my radio messages, sermons, and books. Trace the ancestry of my lessons to their beginning, and you'll find a humpbacked punctuation mark: "Max, can I ask you something?"

Like autumn leaves on soil, these wonderings tend to sit and sink in until springtime emerges and I have a thought or two.

This book collects some of those thoughts.

Many of these answers appeared initially in earlier books. Others are only now pageworthy. But all of them, I pray, will help you with your questions.

By the way, thanks. Thank you for your questions, letters, e-mails, and phone calls. Many of you have opened the door to your heartaches and concerns. You've told me your struggles and shared your joys. You've welcomed me into your lives. I am honored to walk the path with you. After all, aren't we in this together? (Another good question.)

—Max Lucado
San Antonio
Autumn 2010

Hope

—

God, Grace,
and "Why am I here?"

Dear Kelly,

Guilt is not what God wants for his children. When repentance occurs in the heart of the believer, forgiveness is extended by the Father.

Think of it this way: when grace moves in, guilt moves out. God has forgiven us. There is no reason to hold on to guilt —

Max

1. I've been disappointed so many times by human love, and I think this has given me a faulty view of God's love. Can you help me understand how his love is different from human love?

Human love is convenient. It suits the needs of the person at the time and works into his schedule.

God's love is eternal. You are always on God's itinerary. Come and go as you wish, but he's always there.

Human love is limited. It can love only as much as it wants to give.

God's love is unlimited. He has ample amounts of love and even uses words like *abundant* when talking about pouring out his love on people.

Human love is emotional. Feelings dominate a human's love landscape. We feel as though we're in love, or we don't feel as though we're in love. Hormones, sleeplessness, worry, past hurts, Mexican food—all complicate these emotions.

God's love is committed. While God has feelings for us, his feelings don't dictate his love. His love is based on a decision to love us. Your actions don't increase or decrease his commitment. His love is a deeper and more secure love than the fluctuating Ferris wheel of feeling.

Human love is selfish. It must suit our needs and be there for us. To love, we must be loved.

God's love is unselfish. In fact, if you never love God, he will still love you. Your love has no bearing on the amount of love he lavishes on you.

One thing human love has going for it is that you can see it—in the twinkling of your father's eye, in the smile of a spouse, in the joy in your children's voices.

God's love is just as real but not as tangible. We will see it, in time and for eternity, as we gaze at the face of God and his Son, Jesus Christ, while we stand in his presence in heaven.

Our goal as Christians should be to express God's love in our human relationships so people will never make the statement you made. We should all have someone in our lives on whom we can look back and say, "I saw God's love in that person."

2. SOME DAYS I DOUBT GOD. I DOUBT HIS GOODNESS, HIS NEARNESS—
AND THAT HE EVEN EXISTS. WHEN I DOUBT HIM, DOES HE LEAVE ME?

When I was seven years old, I ran away from home. I'd had enough of my father's rules and decided I could make it on my own, thank you very much. With my clothes in a paper bag, I stormed out the back gate and marched down the alley. Like the prodigal son, I decided I needed no father. Unlike the prodigal son, I didn't go far. I got to the end of the alley and remembered I was hungry, so I went back home.

Though the rebellion was brief, it was rebellion nonetheless. Had you stopped me on that prodigal path and asked me who my father was, I just might have said, "I don't need a father. I'm too big for the rules of my family. It's just me, myself, and my paper bag." I don't remember saying that to anyone, but I remember thinking it. And I also remember rather sheepishly stepping in the back door and taking my seat at the supper table across from the very father I had, only moments before, disowned.

Did Dad know of my insurrection? I suspect he did. Did he know of my denial? Fathers usually do. Was I still his son? Apparently so. (No one else was sitting in my place at the table.) Suppose, after speaking to me, you had gone to my father and asked, "Mr. Lucado, your son says he has no need of a father. Do you still consider him your son?" What do you think my dad would have said?

I don't have to guess at his answer. He called himself my father even when I didn't call myself his son. His commitment to me was greater than my commitment to him.

So is God's.

Our God is no fair-weather Father. He's not into this love-'em-and-leave-'em stuff. I can count on him to be in my corner no matter how I perform. You can too.

3. WHO IS GOD? HOW CAN I KNOW WHAT HE IS LIKE? HOW CAN I TRUST THAT HE IS POWERFUL ENOUGH TO TAKE CARE OF ME?

Who is God? How much time do you have?

God is unchanging. The weather changes. Fashion changes. Even change changes. God has not changed and cannot and will not ever change. He is always the same—yesterday, today, and tomorrow (Heb. 6:17–18).

God is unparalleled. Nobody comes close to his power, creativity, wisdom, or love. Many arrogantly believe they are close, but all fall short. There is no one like him (Isa. 40:13–14).

God is ungoverned. You and I have policemen, security guards, politicians, and homeowners' association board members telling us what to do. Not God. He holds the position of King of all kings (1 Tim. 6:15–16).

God is unbelievable. Writers (like myself) try to encapsulate God with a thesaurus of adjectives, but still our fingers freeze up on the keyboard (as mine are now). He's just so . . . well . . . (Job 11:7–8).

God is untouched. One wayward sneeze in my direction, and I am contaminated, sick with a cold and out for a week. No one can soil or stain God. No outbreak of sin can contaminate him. God is holy and righteous, no matter how sick the world gets (1 Sam. 2:2).

God is uncaused. God has no "Made in . . ." stickers on his side. No birthday. No childhood. No influences listed on his résumé. Since no one put God in power, no one can take him out (Ps. 90:1–2).

God is unlimited. We are limited by brain capacity, time, relationship overload, responsibilities (one can be at only one baseball practice at a time), and patience. God has no limit to his time, power, knowledge, and love (Ps. 147:4–5).

So can God take care of you?

I'll let you answer that.

4. I'M BEGINNING TO DOUBT SOME OF THE THINGS I'VE ALWAYS JUST TAKEN FOR GRANTED. LIKE WHETHER THERE REALLY IS A GOD. HOW CAN WE KNOW HE TRULY EXISTS? CAN I KNOW HE'S NOT JUST A PRODUCT OF MY IMAGINATION?

Belief in God is not blind faith. Belief means having a firm conviction ("I believe this to be true"), not hoping it's true ("I believe the Cubs will win the World Series"). It's the kind of assurance you get standing on a huge rock. So how can people get to that place in their belief in God?

Space: Look to the skies. Two hundred billion stars just in the Milky Way galaxy. Billions of galaxies and expanding. Where does it end? How did it all begin?

Earth: Look to creation. So many varieties. So much beauty. A circle of life. How did it all come to be? Why does it work in perfect synchronicity?

Ethics: Look to our morals. A common sense of right and wrong shared by people in different countries and different times in history. Murder is always bad. Courage is always good. Who programmed us?

Bible: Look to God's Word. Examine the wisdom. Experience the stories. Trace its preservation throughout time. How did it remain so well intact despite wars and opposition?

Empty tomb: Look to the resurrection. So many of those who claimed to have seen the risen Lord died with that testimony on their lips. Would they die for a lie? Or did they believe they, too, would rise?

Jesus: Look to him. No other man in history has caused so many questions, stirred so many hearts, given so many answers. Could he be who he said he was?

God is not a product of your imagination. He's far more than any of us could imagine, and he is truth.

5.

MY FIANCÉE AND I STAYED UP LATE LAST NIGHT DISCUSSING THE MEANING OF SIN AND THE NEED FOR SALVATION. WE REALLY HAVE TWO DIFFERENT VIEWPOINTS. ISN'T SIN A VIOLATION OF THE CONSCIENCE?

Actually, it is much more. One of the clearest verses on this question is Romans 3:23: "All have sinned and fall short of the glory of God."

Note the phrase *fall short of.* All of us know what it means to have a shortfall. Sometimes we think of a shortfall in athletic terms. The pole-vaulter doesn't have the strength to jump over the bar, so he falls short. We also think of a shortfall in financial terms. When we have month left at the end of our money rather than money at the end of our month, we suffer a shortfall. According to the Bible, there is another type of shortfall. We don't just fall short athletically or financially but, much more important, spiritually. We fall short of the high standard. We have inadequate goodness in our morality account. Heaven is a holy place, and "those who are not holy will not see the Lord" (Heb. 12:14 NLT).

Simply put, we are not good enough to go to heaven.

So what can we do? Well, we can start doing good deeds. Perhaps if we do enough good deeds, they will offset our bad deeds. The question then surfaces, how many good deeds do we need to do? If I lose my temper in traffic, can I make up for it by waving at the next four cars? If I spend one year being greedy, how many years should I be generous? If I miss church one Sunday, how many services do I have to attend to break even?

No one knows the answer to those questions. No one knows how many good deeds it takes to offset the bad. A rule sheet can't be found. A code has not been discovered. It has not been discovered simply because it doesn't exist. God doesn't operate this way.

Is God nothing more than a heavenly deal broker who barters packages of grace? Does he spend his time on the phone with sinners, saying, "All right, I'll forgive your selfishness if you'll put two dollars in the plate and have your mother-in-law over for dinner"? Is that the kind of God we have? It's certainly not the kind of God we read about in the Bible.

God has been so kind to us. We have no way of balancing the scales. All we can do is ask for mercy. And God, because of his kindness, gives it. God turned over our sins to his Son. His Son, Jesus Christ, died for our sins. He did what we could not do so that we might become what we dare not dream: citizens of heaven.

6. Why talk to God about my troubles? He can't understand.

According to the Bible he can: "For we have no superhuman High Priest to whom our weaknesses are unintelligible—he himself has shared fully in all our experience of temptation, except that he never sinned" (Heb. 4:15 PHILLIPS).

The writer of Hebrews is adamant almost to the point of redundancy. It's as if he anticipates our objections. It's as if he knows that we will say, "God, it's easy for you up there. You don't know how hard it is from down here." So he boldly proclaims Jesus' ability to understand. Look at the wording again.

He himself. Not an angel. Not an ambassador. Not an emissary. But Jesus himself.

Shared fully. Not partially. Not nearly. Not to a large degree. Entirely! Jesus shared fully.

In all our experience. Every hurt. Each ache. All the stresses and all the strains. No exceptions. No substitutes. Why? So he could sympathize with our weaknesses.

Every page of the Gospels hammers home this crucial principle: God knows how you feel. From the funeral to the factory to the frustration of a demanding schedule. Jesus understands. When you tell God that you've reached your limit, he knows what you mean. When you shake your head at impossible deadlines, he shakes his too. When your plans are interrupted by people who have other plans, he nods in empathy.

He has been there.

He knows how you feel.

7. My question's pretty basic. What are we doing here? I mean, is God up to something? If so, what? Is he taking us somewhere? If so, where?

You are right. A more basic question doesn't exist.

One word works well as an answer: *kingdom.* God is creating a kingdom. He is collecting for himself an eternal populace that will reign with him in the new heaven and the new earth.

Old Testament prophets envisioned a time when God would affirm and establish his rule in a new way: "He will rule from sea to sea and from the River to the ends of the earth . . . All kings will bow down to him and all nations will serve him" (Ps. 72:8, 11).

They promised the earthly arrival of an anointed King, a Messiah, one uniquely related to God to serve as the instrument of his rule. "Your King is coming to you; He is just and having salvation, lowly and riding on a donkey" (Zech. 9:9 NKJV).

It's all about the King and his kingdom. "And this is [God's] plan: At the right time he will bring everything together under the authority of Christ—everything in heaven and on earth" (Eph. 1:10 NLT).

It seems to stack up like this:

~ God created the universe as a habitation for humans.
~ Humans exist to become a citizenry for Jesus, the King.
~ Jesus, the King, came to the earth to purchase (pay for the sins of) his people and invite them to heaven.
~ Those who accept his gift are placed in his family and empowered by his Spirit.
~ He is coming back to reclaim us and his creation and to reign over it forever.

The King and his kingdom. That's why we are here. That's where we are headed. That will be some coronation day, don't you think?

8. WHAT IS THE PURPOSE OF CONFESSION? DOESN'T GOD ALREADY KNOW WHAT I'VE DONE? WHY DOES HE NEED ME TO TELL HIM?

The Greek word for *confession* is the compound term *homologeo, homo* meaning "the same" and *logeo* meaning "to speak." To confess is to speak the same, to agree with. In this case, to agree with God.

This definition not only tells us what confession is; it tells us what confession is not. Confession is not complaining. If I merely recite my problems and tell you how tough my life is, I'm not confessing.

Confession is not blaming. Pointing fingers at others without pointing any at myself may feel good for a while, but it does nothing to remove the conflict within me.

Confession is coming clean with God.

King David did. As if the affair with Bathsheba wasn't enough. As if the murder of her husband wasn't enough. Somehow David danced around the truth. He denied his wrongdoing for at least nine months until the child was born. It took a prophet to bring the truth to the surface, but when he did, David didn't like what he saw (2 Samuel 11:1–12:13).

He waved the white flag. No more combat with God. No more arguing with heaven. He confessed. He came clean with God. What was the result of such honesty?

> I confessed all my sins to you
>> and stopped trying to hide my guilt.
> I said to myself, "I will confess my rebellion to the LORD."
>> And you forgave me! All my guilt is gone. (Ps. 32:5 NLT)

Want to get rid of your guilt? Come clean with God.

9. WHEN MY HUSBAND AND I BECAME THE PARENTS OF A BABY GIRL, WE STARTED TO ATTEND CHURCH. THE PASTOR AND OTHERS HERE TALK ABOUT BEING SAVED, BUT WE REALLY DON'T UNDERSTAND WHAT THAT MEANS. CAN YOU HELP US?

The best answer to your question is found in the Bible's best-known scripture:

> For God so loved the world that he gave his one and only Son, that whoever believes in him shall not perish but have eternal life. (John 3:16)

Why does God want to save us? "God so loved . . ." What parents can stand idly by while their child suffers in agony? Who would watch loved ones step toward a perilous pit and not stop them before they plunged into darkness? God loves us so much he wants to save us . . . from the world, from Satan, from ourselves. The motivation that drives all his actions is love . . . love . . . love . . . love. And his love is directed at you.

How does God save us? "He gave his one and only Son . . ." A payment satisfies a debt. A gift appeases anger. A sacrifice dies in place of the guilty party. God saves us by offering his own sacrifice—his own Son—to pay for our massive debt of sin, to satisfy his immense anger toward our rebellion, and to relieve the burden of our guilt. Only one sacrifice was worthy enough to die for all the sins of all the people of all time. Jesus. He died as a sinless and perfect sacrifice on the cross.

What do we need to do to be saved? "Whoever believes in him . . ." The debt is too big to pay. Working ourselves to death wouldn't be enough. So Jesus, out of love, did all the work for us two thousand years ago on a cross outside the walls of Jerusalem. What must we do? Believe. Believe that Jesus died for you and me. Know that God is satisfied and our sin bill has been paid in full.

What will happen as a result of salvation? "Have eternal life." Jesus' death on the cross paid for our sins. Jesus' resurrection from the tomb promises our eternal life. We are no longer stuck on death row. We will be set free to enjoy life eternal with our Savior himself.

God saves us because he loves us.

God saves us through Jesus Christ.

God saves us when we believe.

God saves us from death.

The only question John 3:16 does not answer is, what about you? Have you been saved?

10. Every Easter our family has the same argument: did Jesus come back from the dead? My dad calls the resurrection a fable. I disagree. How can we know?

No one questions the existence of Jesus. Historically, he lived; he preached; he stirred a following and then was killed. No one questions these facts.

And no one questions the existence of a resurrection story. They may not buy it, but they don't question it exists. Skeptics may chalk it up as a legend or hoax, but everyone believes that the early followers proclaimed that Jesus was raised from the dead.

So the remaining question is this one: "Is the tomb empty?"

There are those who say he never died. Instead, they say a soldier mistakenly lowered his body from the cross, and those who loved him mistakenly put him in the tomb. Honestly. After a whipping that could have killed him, after six hours on the cross, after a spear in his side, could this frail and beaten Jesus spend two nights in a tomb and, on the third day, shove back the rock, overpower the soldiers, and encounter the disciples with such vigor that they believed he was raised from the dead? I don't think so.

Some teach that Jesus' body was stolen by his enemies, the religious leaders of Jerusalem. If so, why didn't they produce it? They could have killed Christianity in its cradle! But they didn't. There are those who say the disciples took the body. Maybe the followers of Jesus staged the resurrection. There is only one problem: the disciples spent the rest of their lives proclaiming the resurrection. Some died for their belief. One might die for a truth, but one will never die for a lie.

What is left? The empty tomb is left.

You don't have to toss common sense out the door to embrace the resurrection of Jesus. In fact, it's just as challenging, or more so, to disprove the resurrection as to prove it.

11. I'VE BEEN HAVING TERRIBLE DOUBTS ABOUT MY SALVATION, WHICH IS CAUSING ME GREAT ANXIETY. I KNOW THE DOUBTS COME FROM SATAN, AND I'VE PRAYED AND ASKED GOD FOR ASSURANCE. BUT HOW CAN I KNOW THAT I AM TRULY SAVED?

According to the Bible, it is possible to "know beyond the shadow of a doubt that you have eternal life" (1 John 5:13 MSG).

How do we know that? "If you confess with your mouth, 'Jesus is Lord,' and believe in your heart that God raised him from the dead, you will be saved" (Rom. 10:9).

First, *confess* that Jesus is Lord. Say it out loud or quietly in your heart—either way. Just mean it.

Then *believe* that Jesus was resurrected. He's not a man in the grave but God in the flesh with the power over death.

Confess and believe . . . and you will have salvation.

Catch what Romans 10:9 does not say—live perfectly, be nice to everyone, don't mess up, don't doubt, always smile . . . and you will be saved. Can't do it. Impossible.

Just confess and believe. Salvation will follow.

It's so easy . . . yet so hard.

God wants us to know we are saved, for saved people are dangerous people, willing to face off with the world, unafraid of the consequences since they know that, whatever happens, they will have eternal life.

"Therefore, there is now no condemnation for those who are in Christ Jesus" (Rom. 8:1). Watch out, world!

12.
I SPENT SEVERAL YEARS OF MY LIFE AWAY FROM GOD. I BECAME A CHRISTIAN AS A YOUNGSTER, BUT WHEN I WAS A TEENAGER, I QUIT GOING TO CHURCH AND READING MY BIBLE. I STOPPED PRAYING TO GOD AND OBEYING HIM. DURING THAT TIME, WAS I SAVED?

Really good question. One that has caused many good Bible students to stay up late at night seeking answers. Here are the ideas that make the most sense to me.

Jesus guarantees the protection of his sheep. Not only does he know them by name, but he says, "I give them eternal life, and they shall never perish; no one can snatch them out of my hand" (John 10:28). "No one" means *no one.* God gives those who trust him "an inheritance that can never perish, spoil or fade" (1 Peter 1:4). They are "kept by Jesus" (Jude 1) and "shielded by God's power" (1 Peter 1:5). God is able to "keep you from falling and to present you before his glorious presence without fault and with great joy" (Jude 24). If he is able to keep us from falling, wouldn't he? He is "not wishing for any to perish" (2 Peter 3:9 NASB).

Salvation is not repeatable. Salvation is not a repeated phenomenon. Scripture contains no example of a person who was saved, then lost, then resaved, then lost again. On-and-off salvation never appears in the Bible.

Family ties sustain us. Once we believe, we are adopted into the family of God. "We are children of God" (Rom. 8:16 NASB). After being placed in a family, we are always in the family. Communion between parent and child may suffer, but the tie remains. By sinning we may step out of the will of God, but we will never step out of the family of God.

Persistent sin shows a lack (not loss) of conversion. John taught that those who withdrew from the community were never saved in the first place. "They went out from us, but they did not really belong to us. For if they had belonged to us, they would have remained with us; but their going showed that none of them belonged to us" (1 John 2:19).

God disciplines disobedient children, but he does not disinherit them (Heb. 12:5). The presence of sin does not imply loss of position. Paul claimed to be the chief of sinners: "Christ Jesus came into the world to save sinners, among whom I am foremost of all" (1 Tim. 1:15 NASB). He did not say, "I was." Paul still sinned but never doubted his salvation. He taught the difference between "position" and "practice." We can be positionally secure while our practice reflects otherwise. The Corinthian church was positionally a sanctified church, but practically its members appeared like people of the world (1 Cor. 3:1).

If works are needed to retain salvation, then salvation is achieved by works. Would God start salvation and turn it over to us to complete it? No. He is the "author and finisher of our faith" (Heb. 12:2 NKJV). To say he is anything else places an unbearable burden on the Christian.

If salvation can be lost through sin, then all are at times lost, because all sin. Salvation, then, becomes a matter of timing. We can only hope God will snatch us into heaven during a saved season. If salvation is forfeitable because of unbelief, aren't we all lost? Who has perfect belief? Worriers don't. The fearful don't. If perfect belief qualifies the saved, who qualifies?

In the end, the great discovery is this: what initially saves you, eternally keeps you. During your years away from God, you lost much: you lost joy, peace, and opportunities to glorify God. But you did not lose your place in heaven.

13.

I KNOW GOD HAS FORGIVEN ME FOR MY PAST SINS, BUT IT'S HARD FOR ME TO FORGIVE MYSELF. I'VE TERMINATED TWO PREGNANCIES THAT HAPPENED OUT OF WEDLOCK. I USED DRUGS FOR YEARS AND REALLY MESSED UP MY LIFE. GOD HAS REDEEMED ME, BUT I STILL FEEL SO ASHAMED FOR MY ACTIONS.

Welcome to the Court of Shame. Look around. See anyone you know? Recognize that judge in the long black robe? It's you. In fact the prosecutor looks pretty familiar. You again, this time wearing a nice Italian suit. Glance over to the jury. Yep. Twelve of you all giving you the evil eye and saying, "Guilty."

When it comes to shame, we are our harshest judges.

Sometimes your shame is private.

Sometimes it's public.

Always it's painful.

After hearing the heart of the adulterous woman, Jesus declared, "I also don't judge you guilty. You may go now, but don't sin anymore" (John 8:11 NCV). If Jesus judged her and found her not guilty, what do you think he says about you?

At times like this, you must ask yourself a question: who makes a better judge—you or Jesus?

We make poor judges. Marred by hurt and humiliation, we don't see the situation clearly. We listen too much to the voices that got us into this mess. The abuser still abuses our self-esteem. We allow the molester to still molest our soul. Our judgments are limited.

Jesus knows the situation inside and out. He sees from every perspective and feels all the pain. He knows when lines were crossed and when motives were just. Jesus is the best judge.

So when he says, "I don't judge you guilty," that verdict is based not on a whim but on a careful examination of all the hearts, all the guilt, and all the genuine repentance.

Jesus says he no longer holds any wrong against you.

So if Jesus declares you not guilty, then who keeps whispering guilt in your ears?

Who do you think?

14. HOW CAN I GET FREE OF THE FEAR THAT GOD MIGHT NOT FORGIVE ME? I'M ALWAYS AFRAID THAT I'M NOT PERFECT ENOUGH.

After we'd been in San Antonio only a short time, I decided I should buy a new jacket for Easter. Where we served in Brazil, no one wore coats and ties, so I didn't have many. Hence, I went to buy one. At the rack I realized I was standing next to a well-known citizen, Red McCombs. He owns car lots and at one time owned an NFL football team in Minnesota.

We exchanged greetings and niceties. He told me about his brother, a pastor. I told him how happy I was to be living in San Antonio. After a moment we returned to our shopping. I selected a jacket, went to the cash register to pay for it, and was told these words by the salesman: "Your jacket has already been paid for. The man you were talking to covered your bill." My first thought was, *Boy, I wish I'd picked out some slacks too.*

Think about what happened to me. I was in debt. Then, all of a sudden, I found that my debt had been paid. I could deny the gift or accept it. The decision was easy. The gift giver had ample resources with which to pay for the coat. I had no reason to doubt his sincerity or ability.

Nor do you. God has ample ability to love and care for you.

Of course, what Jesus did on the cross was far greater than what Mr. McCombs did for me in the store. Jesus took our place. What if my benefactor had offered to trade places with me? Exchange financial statements with me? Swap fortunes with me? He would have inherited my debt, and I would have inherited his abundance.

Through Christ we inherit abundant mercy. Enough to cover a lifetime of mistakes. Jesus, in turn, took on severe poverty. While on the cross, he was robbed of everything—his health, his dignity, his friends, his strength, and, most of all, his God.

Once and for all, he proved his love.

15. I know the Bible says I'm forgiven. But my conscience says I'm not.

Jesus loves us too much to leave us in doubt about his grace. His "perfect love expels all fear" (1 John 4:18 NLT). If God loved with an imperfect love, we would have high cause to worry. Imperfect love keeps a list of sins and consults it often. God keeps no list of our wrongs. His love casts out fear because he casts out our sin!

Tether your heart to this promise, and tighten the knot. "If our heart condemns us, God is greater than our heart, and knows all things" (1 John 3:20 NKJV). When you feel unforgiven, evict the feelings. Emotions don't get a vote. Go back to Scripture. God's Word holds rank over self-criticism and self-doubt.

As Paul told Titus, "God's readiness to give and forgive is now public. Salvation's available for everyone! . . . Tell them all this. Build up their *courage*" (Titus 2:11, 15 MSG, emphasis mine). Do you know God's grace? Then you can love boldly, live robustly. You can swing from trapeze to trapeze; his safety net will break your fall.

Nothing fosters courage like a clear grasp of grace.

And nothing fosters fear like an ignorance of mercy. May I speak candidly? If you haven't accepted God's forgiveness, you are doomed to live in fear. Nothing can deliver you from the gnawing realization that you have disregarded your Maker and disobeyed his instruction. No pill, pep talk, psychiatrist, or possession can set the sinner's heart at ease. You may deaden the fear, but you can't remove it. Only God's grace can.

Have you accepted the forgiveness of Christ? If not, do so. "If we confess our sins, He is faithful and just to forgive us our sins and to cleanse us from all unrighteousness" (1 John 1:9 NKJV). Your prayer can be as simple as this: *Dear Father, I need forgiveness. I admit that I have turned away from you. Please forgive me. I place my soul in your hands and my trust in your grace. Through Jesus I pray, amen.*

Having received God's forgiveness, live forgiven!

16.

IF GOD KNEW IN ADVANCE THAT, AFTER JESUS LEFT HEAVEN FOR A TIME, JESUS WOULD BE REUNITED WITH HIM AND THAT JESUS' DEATH WOULD SAVE HUMANITY, IT DOESN'T REALLY SEEM LIKE A SACRIFICE TO ME. WHAT DID GOD GIVE UP?

I've considered this question, not just since your inquiry but for much of my life. Exactly what did God give up when he gave his Son to the world?

I've decided I cannot know. Why? Because I have never been to heaven. When God gave us his Son, his Son gave up heaven. Try to imagine that sacrifice. What if you were to leave your home and become homeless or leave the human race and become a mosquito or a wasp? Would that be comparable to God's becoming human? Jesus, whose address in heaven was Everywhere, limited himself to a human body in a map-dot town on the fringe of the Roman Empire.

Of course, as you said, he did this "for a time." Maybe that is part of the sacrifice. God is timeless, unbound by clocks or calendars. And for a time he entered time.

But as I said, I've never lived in heaven, and I've never been eternal, so I can't understand what he gave up.

Nor have I been sinless, so I can't imagine what it was like to become sin. This is the heart of the Christian gospel. That he who had no sin took on sin (2 Cor. 5:21). That Christ on the cross became a sinner in the eyes of heaven. That he experienced the pain and punishment due to every rapist, thief, mass murderer, and despot.

He paid the price for sin by becoming a sinner. Since I've always been a sinner, I can't appreciate this sacrifice.

And I've never given my child for evil people. I might give myself or a bit of myself to help evil people. But sacrifice one of my daughters? No way. Even if I knew I would see her again, I wouldn't do it. But God did.

It seems to me that God gave more than we could ever ask.

17. My uncle lived like the devil and made life miserable for my parents, who are godly, humble people. My dad tells me that my uncle got saved just a few hours before he died. Can such an awful person be saved on his deathbed after doing so many terrible things?

Jesus told a parable about workers in a vineyard (Matt. 20). Some got hired at the crack of dawn. Others around midmorning. Still others around noon, late afternoon, and then at sunset. All of them received a day's salary.

The early-birds-who-got-the-worm were not happy with this. They wanted the boss to either pay the latecomers less or pay the early risers more. Not all workers deserve to get the same wage, do they? The landowner replied:

> Friend, I am not being unfair to you. Didn't you agree to work for a denarius?[1]
> Take your pay and go. I want to give the man who was hired last the same as
> I gave you. Don't I have the right to do what I want with my own money? Or
> are you envious because I am generous? (Matt. 20:13–15)

When we accept salvation from Jesus Christ, we all accept the same deal—eternal life with the Savior of our soul.

So if someone accepts Christ at ten years old or at the age of eighty-five, lying on his deathbed . . . what's the difference?

God has the right to give the full amount of salvation to whomever he wants.

Are we envious of his generosity? No! His generosity gave us salvation in the first place. We love his generosity. Don't ever change that, God!

The thief on the cross is the best practical example of that generosity.

> In the same way the robbers who were crucified with him also heaped insults
> on him. (Matt. 27:44)

Both robbers mocked Jesus, hurling insults at him.

Yet as death approached, Luke 23 records a shift. While one thief still cursed, the other defended Christ. What happened? In just a few short hours, the second thief went from angry atheist to repentant sinner. Wasn't Jesus offended, those curse words still ringing in his ears?

Then he said, "Jesus, remember me when you come into your kingdom."

Jesus answered him, "I tell you the truth, today you will be with me in paradise." (vv. 42–43)

Jesus forgave him in the final moments.

The time of forgiveness does not matter. Anytime is the best time to receive Christ and the reward of a lifetime.

18. I find no rest in religion. People talk about church and spirituality as if they are an oasis. In my life, church has been a desert.

You may be confusing Christianity with legalism. Legalism is joyless because legalism is endless. There is always another class to attend, person to teach, mouth to feed. Inmates incarcerated in self-salvation find work but never joy. How could they? They never know when they are finished. Legalism leaches joy.

Grace, however, dispenses peace. The Christian trusts a finished work. I like this quote:

> Gone are the exertions of law-keeping, gone the disciplines and asceticisms of legalism, gone the anxiety that having done everything we might not have done enough. We reach the goal not by the stairs but by the lift . . . God pledges his promised righteousness to those who will stop trying to save themselves.[2]

Grace offers rest. Legalism never does.

19.

I HONESTLY DON'T THINK GOD COULD USE ME. I BELIEVE HE FORGAVE ME AND SAVED ME, BUT I DON'T HAVE ANYTHING TO OFFER HIM.

Don't let Satan convince you of this. He will try. He will tell you that God has an IQ requirement or an entry fee. That he employs only specialists and experts, governments and high-powered personalities. When Satan whispers such lies, dismiss him with this truth: God stampeded the first-century society with sway-backs, not thoroughbreds. Before Jesus came along, the disciples were loading trucks, coaching soccer, and selling Slurpee drinks at the convenience store. Their collars were blue, and their hands were calloused, and there is no evidence that Jesus chose them because they were smarter or nicer than the guy next door. The one thing they had going for them was a willingness to take a step when Jesus said, "Follow me" (Mark 1:16–20).

Are you more dinghy than cruise ship? More stand-in than movie star? More plumber than executive? More blue jeans than blue blood? Congratulations. God changes the world with folks like you.

20. Life is filled with more changes right now than I can handle. I just graduated from high school, I'm moving away to attend college, my boyfriend has left me, and my parents are getting a divorce! I feel as if I'm sinking beneath a sea of change.

Nobody likes change . . . except babies. They cry for a change.

The rest of us like small degrees of change but never dramatic, earth-rocking shifts of patterns and routines.

With change comes fear, insecurity, sorrow, and stress. What's the best solution? Hide and hope it all goes away? Never works. Change finds you.

Your cry of sinking beneath a sea of change reminds me of Peter. He and his pals were sailing on calm waters when all of a sudden a storm hit. The winds changed. The waves rose. Not the kind of change a fisherman desires.

> During the fourth watch of the night Jesus went out to them, walking on the lake. When the disciples saw him walking on the lake, they were terrified. "It's a ghost," they said, and cried out in fear.
>
> But Jesus immediately said to them: "Take courage! It is I. Don't be afraid."
>
> "Lord, if it's you," Peter replied, "tell me to come to you on the water." (Matt. 14:25–28)

When he saw Jesus walking on water, Peter decided to get a little change of scenery, to abandon the ship, and to step out in faith on the water.

The change worked.

> "Come," he said.
>
> Then Peter got down out of the boat, walked on the water and came toward Jesus. (v. 29)

It is possible to walk right over the storms of change. Peter proved it! Unfortunately, one other thing changed. Peter's faith.

> But when he saw the wind, he was afraid and, beginning to sink, cried out, "Lord, save me!"
>
> Immediately Jesus reached out his hand and caught him. "You of little faith," he said, "why did you doubt?" (vv. 30–31)

Can't really blame Peter for the momentary lapse of security. The wind and waves were scary.

If only Peter had relied on Jesus' strength . . . *Don't be afraid.*

If only Peter had trusted Jesus' command . . . *Come.*

If only Peter had stayed faithful . . . *Why doubt?*

Peter could have walked right over that sea of change.

One thing to remember: As Peter sank, he cried out, "Lord, save me!" He knew where to find help.

And Jesus reached out his hand to catch Peter.

That's another thing that never changes. Jesus is always there to pull us to safety.

21. MY DAD WAS A VERY IMPATIENT MAN. HE COULD MAKE LIFE DOWNRIGHT MISERABLE FOR EVERYONE AROUND HIM. I THINK I'M BECOMING MORE AND MORE LIKE HIM, AS I'M OFTEN IMPATIENT WITH OTHERS. I DON'T WANT TO BE LIKE THAT. WHAT CAN I DO?

You've heard the saying "A watched pot never boils." Well, it does boil, whether you watch it or not. It just doesn't seem to boil fast enough if you're watching. The saying should go like this: "A watched pot makes you boiling mad while you wait for it to boil."

Impatience wants boiling water *now*! You curse the manufacturer of the pan, bang your fist against those oven bureaucrats, angrily defy the flame, and attack the properties of water! But the only thing you can do is turn up the flame. More flame equals faster boil. Burn, baby, burn!

Patience is a slow boil. It doesn't turn up the flame. It waits for the burner to heat the pan, which heats the water to 212 degrees. This takes some time, and you accept that. You can't change the law of heat transference. So you sit back and allow it to happen.

Both situations want the same thing: boiling water. One is willing to wait. The other will use any means necessary to get it done now, including spontaneous combustion.

Impatience is selfishness with time. We don't like to waste it. People get in our way and slow things down, so we burn them with impatience!

The Greek word for *patience* means "taking a long time to boil." Patience recognizes that we share time with others—it's not just our time. Patience knows other factors are at work in this world and we need to adjust to their time schedules too. Some things can be sped up (with encouragement, not flames of retribution). Some things can't.

The best way to turn down the flame is with love.

"Love is patient" (1 Cor. 13:4).

Love forgives laziness. Love understands people's weaknesses. Love wants the best for everyone. Love is a relationship, not a means to an end.

Love is a fruit hanging from the tree of Galatians 5:22. It's the first fruit and some say the most important. The seeds of love produce the harvest of all the other fruits: joy, peace, patience . . .

If you have the Holy Spirit, then you have the potential of making patience a part of your life. Thankfully, God is patient while you find that patience.

22. I HAVE TO ADMIT I'M NOT LOOKING FORWARD TO GROWING OLD. I'VE WORKED IN A NURSING HOME FOR YEARS, AND THIS HAS ONLY MADE ME DREAD OLD AGE. THIS ATTITUDE DOESN'T SEEM TO BE RATIONAL, BUT I CAN'T SEEM TO ACCEPT THE INEVITABLE.

> Altogether, Abraham lived a hundred and seventy-five years. Then Abraham breathed his last and died at a good old age, an old man and full of years; and he was gathered to his people. (Gen. 25:7–8)

There's an expression in the Bible that has always fascinated me. When referring to someone's death, it says he died "full of years."

It's used to describe Abraham, Isaac, and Job.

"Full of years" could mean lots of years. Abraham and Isaac lived two of our lifetimes. That's a lot of years.

It could also express the idea that the years of their lives were full, busy with God's packed agenda. Maybe it means they died fulfilling all they set out to accomplish.

I don't know if I would want to live 180 years, but I know I want to live all the years of my life as if they were the last and do everything I can to make sure they fulfill all God wants me to do.

I want to die fulfilled, having done everything I could with the time I had. If I'm in a nursing home, I want to lead Bible studies, Beatles sing-alongs, and square dances and make sure every resident there has a personal relationship with Christ while the synapses in my brain are still sparking and my hip bones are strong.

Getting old is inevitable. But are you going to hobble and groan your way to the grave or race your rickety old wheelchair downhill to your funeral? We're all going to end up the same way, but we can have fun getting there!

23.
CAN OUR LIVES COUNT FOR CHRIST IF WE DON'T HAVE THE CALLING TO BE A MINISTER? I TRY TO BE FAITHFUL IN TELLING OTHERS ABOUT SALVATION, ESPECIALLY MY GRANDCHILDREN. DO YOU THINK THIS MATTERS IN THE LONG RUN?

Sounds as if you are doing exactly what a minister does. Paul says in Romans 15:15–20:

> . . . because of the grace God gave me to be a minister of Christ Jesus to the Gentiles with the priestly duty of proclaiming the gospel of God, so that the Gentiles might become an offering acceptable to God, sanctified by the Holy Spirit.
>
> Therefore I glory in Christ Jesus in my service to God. I will not venture to speak of anything except what Christ has accomplished through me in leading the Gentiles to obey God by what I have said and done—by the power of signs and miracles, through the power of the Spirit. So from Jerusalem all the way around to Illyricum, I have fully proclaimed the gospel of Christ. It has always been my ambition to preach the gospel where Christ was not known.

You don't have to put a collar around your neck, eat at every potluck dinner that comes around, or preach long, boring sermons to be a minister.

According to Paul, ministers

~ proclaim the gospel everywhere they go, and
~ testify to God's work in their lives.

Paul made a difference. Sounds as if you do too.

Will it matter?

When you arrive in heaven, I wonder if Christ might say these words to you: "I'm so proud that you let me use you. Because of you, others are here today. Would you like to meet them?"

Neighbors, coworkers, friends, strangers, and family members (parents, spouse, children, grandchildren) all step forward.

Even great-grandchildren, whom you never met, are there because you ministered to your kids and to your grandchildren.

Does ministering make a difference? Yes.

Are you a minister? You bet.

Are you making a difference? Absolutely.

And while you're at it, eat at every potluck you can.

24.
I SUFFER FROM UNANSWERED PRAYERS. WHAT I ASK GOD TO DO AND WHAT HE DOES ARE TWO DIFFERENT THINGS.

Think for a moment about God's priority. *God exists to showcase God.*

Why do the heavens exist? The heavens exist to "declare the glory of God" (Ps. 19:1).

Why did God choose the Israelites? Through Isaiah he summoned "everyone who is called by My name, whom I have created for My glory" (Isa. 43:7 NKJV).

Why do people struggle? God answers, "I have tested you in the furnace of affliction. For My own sake, for My own sake, I will act" (Isa. 48:10–11 NASB). "Call on me when you are in trouble, and I will rescue you, and you will give me glory" (Ps. 50:15 NLT).

God has one goal: God. To proclaim his glory.

God has no ego problem. *He does not reveal his glory for his good. We need to witness it for our good.*

He responds to our prayers with this goal in mind. If he says no to our requests, it is because his glory matters more than our preferences.

25. YESTERDAY I APPLIED FOR A JOB THAT SEEMED TO BE GOD'S PLAN FOR ME. TODAY I'M WONDERING WHETHER AN INTERNSHIP ABROAD MIGHT BE HIS PLAN INSTEAD. HOW DO I KNOW WHICH IS THE RIGHT THING TO DO?

The Lord has assigned to each his task. (1 Cor. 3:5)

Like a pilot before takeoff, I always go over my preflight checklist before I take any trips into the unknown. I ask myself:

Where has God taken me before? I look at my passport, remembering all the exciting and adventurous places God has sent me in the past. I remember the experiences I faced, the cultures I embraced, the lifestyles I encountered. Then I consider how often God uprooted folks in Scripture. Who better to confront Pharaoh than an Egyptian-raised Jew? Who better to lead Israel than a shepherd-trained warrior? Who better to bridge the gap between deep thinkers and deep believers than a Roman-trained ex-Pharisee? God uses past experiences to overcome present problems.

Ask yourself, where has God taken me before?

What trips am I passionate about? Some people get excited about going to Hawaii. Others, Toledo. Many think Alaska is too cold. Others feel the Bahamas are too hot. We all have different passions and burdens. Some like to preach in foreign countries. Others like to help their neighbors. Some hurt for gang members and drug dealers. Others weep over Wall Street and Capitol Hill.

Ask yourself, what people and places am I most passionate about?

Am I a pilot, a flight attendant, a mechanic, or a baggage handler? I never see the pilot percolating coffee or the attendant with a screwdriver under the airplane's hood. Why? Because we all have something we are good at, and we are expected to do that one thing well. Pilots take people places. Flight attendants serve. Mechanics make sure everything is working well behind the scenes. Baggage handlers carry other people's burdens.

Think about it: what is your purpose?

Once you've checked off the . . .

~ previous places,
~ present passions,
~ professional purpose,

you are ready to fly!

26. I WANT TO BECOME A DOCTOR AND WORK WITH THE POOR, BUT THIS SEEMS LIKE AN IMPOSSIBLE DREAM. MY HEART TELLS ME THIS DREAM IS FROM GOD, BUT MY PARENTS THINK I'M BEING FOOLISH. HOW DO I KEEP THEIR DOUBTS FROM DESTROYING MY DREAM?

Let's be honest—there's a lot in life that doesn't make sense.

School. Friends. The news. Politics. Wall Street. Even God's track record in the Bible doesn't make a lot of sense:

~ Transporting a million or so people across the desert for forty years to a mysterious promised land (Exodus–Deuteronomy)
~ Whittling a thirty-two-thousand-man army down to three hundred in order to attack the most feared warriors in the land, then arming the three hundred men with trumpets, jars, and torches (Judg. 7:1–16)
~ Saving the world through a baby born in a barn (Luke 2:1–7)
~ Spreading the gospel to the world with twelve imperfect men—a treasurer who took bribes, a confidant who denied Jesus, and another who preferred to run away naked than get captured (Matt. 26:14–16; John 12:4–6; Matt. 26:69–75; Mark 14:51–52)

So if someone has a dream that makes perfect sense, it really couldn't be from God. That's not how he dreams!

We forget that *impossible* is one of God's favorite words. He dreams impossible dreams. Why?

If you accomplish a possible dream, then you get all the glory.

But if you accomplish an impossible dream, then God gets all the glory.

The purpose of impossible dreams is to show the world that an incredible, unbelievable God still exists, and he works in the lives of people.

And it all begins with dreams like yours of reaching the poor and destitute.

While it may seem your parents are dousing your passion with doubt, they could be injecting some much-needed wisdom into your plans for fulfilling your dream. Your parents do love you and want to ensure you make the best decision. So listen to them. Practicality and logic aren't all bad. Doubt may be caution in disguise.

In the end you must ask yourself, whose dream am I going to follow: mine, my parents', or God's? God's dreams are always bigger and better and more unbelievable. His dreams look like these:

~ Your neighbors . . . your community . . . your school coming to Christ
~ Churches in your zip code coming together to pray for revival
~ An end to hunger and disease in just one country
~ Peace on earth

Dare to dream like God.

27. Is God willing to use anyone to change the world? Even people who've lived ungodly lives?

I hope so. If God chose only righteous people to change the world, you could count them all on one finger—Jesus. Instead, he included others in his plan—the sinners, the ungodly, the imperfect, the fearful, the prideful, the truth twisters. There's a lot more of us to choose from.

People like

~ Abraham—liar
~ Jacob—deceiver
~ Moses—murderer, excuse maker
~ David—adulterer, murderer
~ Solomon—worldly, adulterer
~ Elijah—pouting prophet
~ Gomer and Rahab—prostitutes
~ Matthew—tax collector
~ Peter—denier with anger issues

The reassuring lesson is clear. God used (and uses!) people to change the world. People! Not saints or superhumans or geniuses but people. Crooks, creeps, lovers, and liars—he uses them all. And what they lack in perfection, God makes up for in love.

If you ever wonder how God can use you to make a difference in your world, just look at those he has already used, and take heart. No matter who you are or what you've done, God can use you.

Because you're imperfect, you can speak of making mistakes.

Because you're a sinner, you can speak of forgiveness.

God restores the broken and the brittle, then parades them before the world as trophies of his love and strength. The world sees the ungodly turn godly, and they know God must love them too.

28. Can God use his followers today as he did his first followers? I keep hearing this is what should make us stand out from non-Christians, but I don't think we even begin to compare to those early believers. Why not?

Ours is the wealthiest generation of Christians ever. We are bright, educated, and experienced. We can travel around the world in twenty-four hours or send a message in a millisecond. We have the most sophisticated research and medicines at the tips of our fingers. We have ample resources. A mere 2 percent of the world's grain harvest would be enough, if shared, to erase the problems of hunger and malnutrition around the world.[3] There is enough food on the planet to offer every person twenty-five hundred calories of sustenance a day.[4] We have enough food to feed the hungry.

And we have enough bedrooms to house the orphans. Here's the math. There are 145 million orphans worldwide.[5] Nearly 236 million people in the United States call themselves Christians.[6] From a purely statistical standpoint, American Christians by themselves have the wherewithal to house every orphan in the world.

I don't mean to oversimplify these terribly complicated issues. We can't just snap our fingers and expect the grain to flow across borders or governments to permit foreign adoptions. Policies stalemate the best of efforts. International relations are strained. Corrupt officials snag the systems. I get that.

But this much is clear: the storehouse is stocked. The problem is not in the supply; the problem is in the distribution. God has given this generation, our generation, everything we need to alter the course of human suffering.

The problem is not information; the problem is dissemination. We have a complete Bible with all the scripture needed to teach the world and the means to distribute that message verbally, electronically, and in 3-D.

Change needs to begin with the Christians today—just as it started two thousand years ago with the transformation of the apostles, who gave up everything to take the gospel everywhere.

We can be two thousand times more effective, if we only try.

29. How should I react to poverty? It seems like a huge problem.

Some people are poor because they are lazy. They need to get off their duffs. Others, however, are poor because parasites weaken their bodies, or they spend six hours a day collecting water, or rebel armies ravaged their farms, or AIDS took their parents.

Couldn't such people use a bit of help?

Of course they could. So . . .

Let the church act on behalf of the poor. The apostles did. "So the Twelve called a meeting of all the believers" (Acts 6:2 NLT). They assembled the entire church. The problem of inequity warranted a churchwide conversation. The leaders wanted every member to know that this church took poverty seriously. The ultimate solution to poverty is found in the compassion of God's people. Scripture endorses not forced communism but Spirit-led volunteerism among God's people.

Let the brightest among us direct us. "And so, brothers, select seven men who are well respected and are full of the Spirit and wisdom. We will give them this responsibility" (v. 3 NLT).

The first church meeting led to the first task force. The apostles unleashed their best people on their biggest problem. The challenge demands this. "Poverty," as Rich Stearns, president of World Vision in the United States, told me, "is *rocket science.*" Simple solutions simply don't exist. Most of us don't know what to do about the avalanche of national debt, the withholding of lifesaving medicines, the corruption at the seaports, and the abduction of children. Most of us don't know what to do, but someone does!

And one more idea. *Get ticked off.* Riled up enough to respond. Righteous anger would do a world of good. Poverty is not the lack of charity but the lack of justice. Why do a billion people go to bed hungry every night?[7] Why do nearly thirty thousand children die every day, one every three seconds, from hunger and preventable diseases?[8] It's just not fair. Why not do something about it?

No one can do everything, but everyone can do something.

30. DOES REPENTANCE OCCUR WHEN A PERSON COMES TO CHRIST OR AS A PERSON GROWS IN CHRIST?

The answer is yes.

When we come to Christ, we turn away from the old life. If we were living in adultery, we get out. If we were cheating on our taxes, we stop. If we were boasting about self, we begin boasting about Christ. Everything we know to do, we try to do.

The problem, however, is that we don't know everything to do. The longer we hang out with Jesus, the more we see what needs to change. Repentance becomes more than an event. It becomes a lifestyle.

My college roommate, Steve Green, was neat. Not just neat in the sense of a lot of fun but neat in the sense of not sloppy. I, on the other hand, tend to be sloppy. Why make up a bed you're going to sleep in that night?

Before going to college, I promised my mom that I would be neater. And I kept my promise. I repented of my sloppy ways. But when I saw the way Steve lived, I realized that my repentance had a long way to go. One look at our room and you saw the contrast. On his side of the room, you could eat off the floor. On my side of the room, you couldn't see the floor.

Now, Steve was very gracious. He didn't demand that I change, but little by little he helped me change. Every few days I learned something new. I learned the purpose of hangers. The reason for toothpaste lids. I learned that underwear should be worn only once between washings. Our four years of rooming together were four years of regular repentance. Then he turned me over to Denalyn, and she is still working on me.

The same thing happens to the Christian. When he comes to Christ, he repents. But as Christ moves in and takes up residence in his life, he sees how sloppy he is. And, over time, his language changes. His habits change. His money management changes. He lives a lifestyle of repentance.

We are always cleaning up our act.

Hurt

Conflicts, Calamities,
and "Why me?"

Dear Amy,

God must love you very much.
He entrusted you with Madison,
a special child. She needed
a mom with a deep heart
and a rock-solid faith. For
whatever time Madison has
on earth, she will see Jesus
in you. You can be Jesus in
her life. What a gift you
are able to give her!

May God grant healing, strength
and peace —

Max

31.

I WORK IN A CANCER HOSPITAL. I SEE PATIENTS, ESPECIALLY CHILDREN, WHO PRAY EVERY DAY FOR MIRACLES. THEY STRUGGLE SO MUCH. WHAT CAN I TELL THEM?

Tell them that God uses struggles for his glory. The last three years of my dad's life were scarred by ALS, amyotrophic lateral sclerosis. The disease took him from being a healthy mechanic to being a bed-bound paralytic. He lost his voice and his muscles, but he never lost his faith. Visitors noticed. Not so much in what he said but more in what he didn't say. Never outwardly angry or bitter, Jack Lucado suffered with dignity.

His faith led one man to seek a like faith. After my dad's funeral this man sought me out and told me. Because of my dad's example, he became a Jesus follower. Did God orchestrate my father's illness for that very reason?

Knowing the value he places on one soul, I wouldn't be surprised. And imagining the splendor of heaven, I know my father's not complaining.

A season of suffering is a small assignment when compared to the reward.

32.
I JUST SPENT THE AFTERNOON AT THE HOSPITAL BEDSIDE OF A
DEAR FRIEND. SHE JUST GAVE BIRTH, AND HER BABY WAS BORN
WITH ONE FOOT. WHAT PURPOSE DOES THIS SERVE? HOW CAN A GOOD
GOD PERMIT SUCH DEFORMITIES?

Some seasons make no sense. Who can find a place in life's puzzle for the deformity of a child or the enormity of an earthquake's devastation? Do such occurrences serve a purpose?

It helps to see them from an eternal perspective. What makes no sense in this life will make perfect sense in the next. I have proof: you in the womb.

I know you don't remember this prenatal season, so let me remind you what happened. Every gestation day equipped you for your earthly life. Your bones solidified, your eyes developed, the umbilical cord transported nutrients into your growing frame . . . for what reason? So you might remain enwombed? Quite the contrary. Womb time equipped you for earth time, suited you up for your postpartum existence.

Some prenatal features went unused before birth. You grew a nose but didn't breathe. Eyes developed, but could you see? Your tongue, toenails, and crop of hair served no function in your mother's belly. But aren't you glad you have them now?

Certain chapters in this life seem so unnecessary, like nostrils on the preborn. Suffering. Loneliness. Disease. Holocausts. Martyrdom. If we assume this world exists just for pregrave happiness, these atrocities disqualify it from doing so. But what if this earth is the womb? Might these challenges, severe as they are, serve to prepare us, equip us for the world to come? As Paul wrote, "These little troubles are *getting us ready* for an eternal glory that will make all our troubles seem like nothing" (2 Cor. 4:17 CEV, emphasis mine).

33.
MY PASTOR OFFERS TO VISIT THE SICK AND ANOINT THEM WITH OIL. SOUNDS LIKE VOODOO TO ME. WHAT DO YOU THINK?

Sounds to me like your pastor is reading the Bible.

> Anyone who is having troubles should pray. Anyone who is happy should sing praises. Anyone who is sick should call the church's elders. They should pray for and pour oil on the person in the name of the Lord. And the prayer that is said with faith will make the sick person well; the Lord will heal that person. And if the person has sinned, the sins will be forgiven. Confess your sins to each other and pray for each other so God can heal you. When a believing person prays, great things happen. (James 5:13–16 NCV)

James envisions a person in need of help. A body in pain, a mind in torment, even a heart broken. His prescription? The prayers, touch, and tears of an elder. The suffering person is not told to call a friend, deacon, evangelist, or miracle worker; he is told to call an elder. He's not told to attend a rally or a seminar or a crusade; he is told to seek his spiritual shepherds. James urges the suffering member to call elders. It's a voluntary step. No coercion. No persuasion. A wounded sheep calls his shepherds, and they come to pray.

This verse is the earliest mention of elders in the Christian church. It is no coincidence that the earliest mention of elders involves prayer. Prayer is their chief function. Just as the apostles gave themselves intently to pray and teach the Word of God (Acts 6:4), so the elders are to do the same today. No feeble prayer, not memorized prayer, but faithful prayer. Prayer rooted in the faith that God is good and he will do what is right.

As a part of their time with the ill, elders hear their honest confessions. The healing of the soul and the body are interrelated. James understood that the culprit behind many physical conditions is unresolved spiritual issues. How many hospital beds are occupied because of guilt, worry, anger, hatred, bigotry? Many are sick, not because of an infection, but because of a defection of the Spirit.

Consider the power of this moment! A willing member in honest confession submits to the thunderbolt of prayerful elders.

As the elders pray for the sick, they anoint them with oil. In the Old Testament, oil represented the presence of the Holy Spirit. When a person is touched with oil, two wonderful things occur. First, the power of the Holy Spirit is sought, and, second, the sick person is touched.

If you have ever endured a lengthy illness, you know the significance of human touch. If you have studied the Bible, you know the preeminence of laying on of hands. Jesus often associated laying on of hands with healing. He laid his hands on the man at Bethsaida twice before he fully recovered his sight (Mark 8:22–25). On the island of Malta the apostle Paul laid hands on the sick, and they were healed (Acts 28:7–10). Jesus said of his followers, they will touch the sick, and they will be healed (Mark 16:18).

Healing prayer should neither be elevated nor neglected, neither worshipped nor dismissed. Healing prayer should be a normal part of living each day under the reign of God.

34. I GET TIRED OF HEARING PEOPLE BRUSH ASIDE TROUBLES WITH THE PLATITUDE "ALL THINGS WORK TOGETHER FOR GOOD." THIS SEEMS CRUEL TO ME, ESPECIALLY WHEN SOME PEOPLE ARE SUFFERING TERRIBLE TRAGEDIES. DO YOU THINK SAYING THINGS LIKE THIS IS CRUEL OR HELPFUL?

You are referencing Romans 8:28: "We know that in everything God works for the good of those who love him" (NCV). And I think it's one of the most helpful, comforting verses of the entire Bible, announcing God's sovereignty in any painful, tragic situation we face.

God works. Paul's word for this is *sunergeo.* The verb is the great-great-grandfather of the contemporary term *synergy.* Paul is saying that God can make all things *sunergeo* for the good. God is active and creative, blending the paprika with the parsley, the faith with the failings, the triumphs with the tears, and the strides with the stumbles. Individually the ingredients may repel. But together they appeal. Why?

Because we know that God is at work *for good.*

God uses our struggles to build character. James makes the same point in his letter. "My brethren, count it all joy when you fall into various trials, knowing that the testing of your faith produces patience. But let patience have its perfect work, that you may be perfect and complete, lacking nothing" (James 1:2–4 NKJV).

Today's trial leads to tomorrow's maturity. Hasn't the oyster taught us this principle? The grain of sand invades the comfort of the shell, and how does the oyster respond? How does he cope with the irritation? Does he go to the oyster bar for a few drinks? Does he get depressed and clam up? Does he go on a shopping binge and shell out a bunch of money to get over the pain? No. He emits the substance that not only overcomes the irritation but also transforms the irritation into a pearl. Every pearl is simply a victory over irritations.

So what do we do in the meantime? We trust. We trust totally, and we remember: "God is working . . . God is working for the good . . . God is using all things."

Any verse can be misused, but that doesn't render it useless. Romans 8:28 was never meant to be a meaningless platitude but to be one of the most meaningful assurances to the weary and brokenhearted of God's sovereignty.

35.

My boss has a habit of making snide comments about me that really hurt. I like my job, but this person keeps tearing down my self-esteem and making life very difficult for me. What can I do?

> When they hurled their insults at [Jesus], he did not retaliate; when he suffered, he made no threats. Instead, he entrusted himself to him who judges justly. (1 Peter 2:23)

Jesus, after hours of put-downs, mockings, and parodies, said nothing. He did not fire back with one sarcastic atomic bomb. And you would have to think, with his mastery of the language and the number of clever verbal assaults he'd heard in his lifetime, he could have made them sweat.

So what are we supposed to do when the boss hurls insults at us?

Did you see what Jesus did not do when the crowds and the guards insulted him? He did not retaliate. He did not bite back. He did not say, "I'll get you!" No, these statements were not found on Christ's lips.

Did you see what Jesus did do? He prayed. He "entrusted himself to him who judges justly." Or said more simply, he left the judging to God. He did not take on the task of seeking revenge. He demanded no apology. He hired no bounty hunters.

Never, never have I seen such love. If ever a person deserved a shot at revenge and had the power to do some serious supernatural damage in the process, Jesus did. But he didn't call down armies. He called down grace. He died for them.

How could he do it? I don't know. But I do know that all of a sudden my wounds seem painless. My grudges and hard feelings are quite petty.

Days later, Jesus rose again, victorious, to eternal life, while the mockers woke up still stewing in their miserable lives—angry, painful, unforgiven, graceless. In the end, truth won out. It always does.

36. I HAVE A SHORT TEMPER AND SEEM TO GET ANGRY AT THE SMALLEST THINGS. I KNOW THIS CAUSES FRICTION IN MY RELATIONSHIPS, AND THAT HURTS. HOW DO I GET OUT OF THIS RUT?

I wonder what formed the Grand Canyon?

Maybe a few drips here and there. A leaky underground faucet or a gentle rain on a peaceful night. Slowly more and more water built up. Thunderstorms. Lightning. Angry expressions from the sky spilling out in the raging river called the Colorado.

Soon this river begins to tear through the earth, eating it away, eroding its past. Clawing and ripping. This once-innocent stream now full of power and purpose. As years go by, the crevasse is dug.

Our anger builds like the Colorado. Slowly, slowly small things drip, drip, drip down, annoying, irritating, finally enraging.

That was mine! Drip.

Get out of my way! Drip.

You do this all the time! Drip.

Why can't I get something for once! Drip.

Don't tell me what to do! Drip.

The pressure and the buildup explodes, unleashing a frenzy of anger, pouring out in our words, sweeping away our loved ones, our homes, and our peace.

Don't wait until you have a gushing fire hydrant. Go after the small drips. Address every little irritant with forgiveness and prayer. Slowly the pressure relaxes, and the gauge decreases from ten to four to three, then two and one.

Do it before your anger digs a canyon in your life . . . with you on one side and everyone you know on the other.

37.
I'M AFRAID TO ENJOY LIFE AND TRY NEW THINGS; I FEEL I'M BEING LAUGHED AT. I'M ALSO AFRAID TO GO PLACES BECAUSE I WORRY THAT I MIGHT GET INTO AN ACCIDENT. SO I HANG OUT IN MY HOUSE IN MY LITTLE TOWN AND NEVER VENTURE TOO FAR AWAY FROM MY COMFORT ZONE. I REALLY DON'T LIKE LIVING THIS WAY.

In my book *Fearless* I wrote:

> When fear shapes our lives, safety becomes our god. When safety becomes our god, we worship the risk-free life. Can the safety lover do anything great? Can the risk-averse accomplish noble deeds? For God? For others? No. The fear-filled cannot love deeply. Love is risky. They cannot give to the poor. Benevolence has no guarantee of return. The fear-filled cannot dream wildly. What if their dreams sputter and fall from the sky? The worship of safety emasculates greatness. No wonder Jesus wages such a war against fear.

The Gospels address fear head-on. The consensus? Don't be afraid.

Afraid of death and satanic forces at work? "Do not be afraid of those who kill the body but cannot kill the soul" (Matt. 10:28).

Afraid of God's calling you into a whole new life? "But the angel said to her, 'Do not be afraid, Mary, you have found favor with God'" (Luke 1:30).

Afraid of the world? "Peace I leave with you; my peace I give you. I do not give to you as the world gives. Do not let your hearts be troubled and do not be afraid" (John 14:27).

Afraid of job loss, foreclosure, and bankruptcy? "Do not be afraid, little flock, for your Father has been pleased to give you the kingdom" (Luke 12:32).

Afraid of what people are saying behind your back? "So do not be afraid of them. There is nothing concealed that will not be disclosed, or hidden that will not be made known" (Matt. 10:26).

Afraid that Jesus has left you? "He [God] Himself has said, I will not in any way fail you nor give you up nor leave you without support. [I will] not, [I will] not, [I will] not in any degree leave you helpless nor forsake nor let [you] down (relax My hold on you)! [Assuredly not!]" (Heb. 13:5 AMPLIFIED BIBLE).

Fear's main goal is to keep you from God's plan for your life, so don't allow it to win.

If anything should be afraid, it should be fear itself.

38.
MY BOSS PROMISED ME A PROMOTION EVERY TIME HE NEEDED ME TO WORK OVERTIME. I WORKED SIXTY-HOUR WEEKS FOR YEARS. BUT WHEN A BIG PROMOTION CAME UP—YOU GUESSED IT—HE PASSED OVER ME FOR A NEW PERSON AT THE COMPANY. I HAVE TO KEEP WORKING WITH THIS BOSS, BUT MY RESENTMENT MAKES IT VERY DIFFICULT FOR ME EVEN TO BE CIVIL WITH HIM.

The boss who promised promotions has forgotten you. And you are hurt.

Part of you is broken, and the other part is bitter. Part of you wants to cry, and part of you wants to fight. The tears you cry are hot because they come from your heart, where there is a fire burning. It's the fire of anger. It's blazing. It's consuming. Its flames leap up under a steaming pot of revenge.

And you are left with a decision. "Do I put out the fire or heat it up? Do I get over it or get even? Do I release it or resent it? Do I let my hurts heal, or do I let hurt turn into hate?"

That's a good definition of resentment: resentment is when you let your hurt become hate. Resentment is when you allow what is eating you to eat you up. Resentment is when you poke, stoke, feed, and fan the fire, stirring the flames and reliving the pain.

Revenge is the raging fire that consumes the arsonist. Bitterness is the trap that snares the hunter.

And mercy is the choice that can set them all free.

"Blessed are the merciful," said Jesus on the mountain. Those who are merciful to others are the ones who are truly blessed. Why? Jesus answered the question: "they will be shown mercy" (Matt. 5:7).

The merciful, says Jesus, are shown mercy. They witness grace. They are blessed because they are testimonies to a greater goodness. Forgiving others allows us to see how God has forgiven us. The dynamic of giving grace is the key to understanding grace, for it is when we forgive others that we begin to feel what God feels.

Because God has forgiven you more than you'll ever be called on to forgive in another, set your enemy—and yourself—free.

39.
My ex-wife and I share joint custody of our kids. She constantly says negative things about me to our kids and seems intent on destroying my relationship with them. I want to keep a positive relationship with her for the sake of the kids, but it's so hard to keep forgiving her.

We forgive the one-time offenders. We dismiss the parking-place takers, the date breakers, and even the purse snatchers.

We can move past the misdemeanors, but the felonies? The repeat offenders?

Vengeance fixes your attention on life's ugliest moments. Score settling freezes your stare at cruel events in your past. Is this where you want to look? Will rehearsing and reliving your hurts make you a better person? By no means. It will destroy you.

Your enemies still figure into God's plan. Their pulse is proof: God hasn't given up on them. They may be out of God's will but not out of his reach. You honor God when you see them not as his failures but as his projects.

God occupies the only seat on the supreme court of heaven. He wears the robe and refuses to share the gavel. For this reason Paul wrote, "Don't insist on getting even; that's not for you to do. 'I'll do the judging,' says God. 'I'll take care of it'" (Rom. 12:19 MSG).

Revenge removes God from the equation. Vigilantes displace and replace God. "I'm not sure you can handle this one, Lord. You may punish too little or too slowly. I'll take this matter into my hands, thank you."

Only God assesses accurate judgments. We impose punishments too slight or too severe. God dispenses perfect justice. Vengeance is his job. Leave your enemies in God's hands. You're not endorsing their misbehavior when you do. You can hate what someone did without letting hatred consume you. Forgiveness is not excusing.

You have an opportunity to teach your children, during your limited time together, a valuable lesson in forgiveness. Revenge and retaliation are not yours. Model for your children the same attitude Jesus showed in his life and on the cross.

40.
A Christian friend of mine tends to be rude to people in the service industry with her comments and actions. I'm offended and embarrassed by her behavior. Am I wrong to be bothered?

We see Jesus dining out a few times in the Bible. What did he do?

At the feedings of the four and five thousand, Jesus played chef and asked the disciples to be the waiters (Matt. 15:29–38; 14:13–21).

While communing with the apostles at Passover, he played host and washed their feet. The host became the servant (John 13:1–17).

While Jesus was eating with the Pharisees, a woman with a sinful past anointed him with priceless oil. Jesus kindly allowed her to interrupt his meal and worship him (Luke 7:36–38).

Jesus was rude to only one group of people while eating—the Pharisees, who spoiled his meal with their distasteful treatment of others (Luke 7:39–50).

So what would Jesus leave a waiter?

Encouragement to help him endure the struggles of his job.

Forgiveness despite the mismatched orders and dirty spoon.

Eternity with a spoken word or an invitation to hear more.

Thanks communicated clearly through a satisfactory gratuity of 15 to 20 percent.

Jesus understood what it meant to be a servant, and he would certainly serve the servants with kindness and respect.

41. I WAS SEXUALLY ABUSED AS A CHILD, AND I'VE HONESTLY TRIED TO FORGIVE THIS PERSON. BUT I CONTINUE TO SUFFER THE EFFECTS OF THE ABUSE, BOTH MENTALLY AND PHYSICALLY, SO THE PAIN AND ANGUISH KEEP ME ON A CRAZY CYCLE. ONE DAY I FEEL THAT I CAN FORGIVE, AND THE NEXT I FEEL I CAN'T.

Your pain is real. No greeting-card homily is going to solve all your problems. But stay with me a moment as I suggest a perspective shift.

Hurt people hurt people. The person who sexually abused you did so because he was hurt at some time. That person refused to forgive his abuser and decided to take out his aggressions on you.

Forgiveness breaks the chain of abuse. Forgiveness resolves the past and protects the future.

Without it you are doomed to pass on abuse. Not necessarily sexually but through anger or a lack of commitment in relationships. Somewhere, sometime, with some unwitting victim, hurt pops unexpectedly out of the box and destroys another party.

Jesus forgave people in the past, present, and future. Imagine forgiving hurt that hasn't even happened to you yet. You don't have a reason to hate someone, but you forgive before he gives you one. A person doesn't repent for something he hasn't yet done, but Jesus has already forgiven him.

Before you get caught in the crazy cycle of hurt and forgivelessness, try shifting your glance away from the one who hurt you and setting your eyes on the One who has saved you.

We all need forgiveness. Especially the person who hurt you.

42.

I BELIEVED IN FORGIVENESS UNTIL OUR EX–SON-IN-LAW BROKE OUR DAUGHTER'S HEART. HE CHEATED ON HER, DROPPED HER, AND NOW IS DEMANDING CUSTODY OF OUR GRANDCHILD. FORGIVENESS? NOT LIKELY.

Some time ago I was speaking about anger at a men's gathering. I described resentment as a prison and pointed out that when we put someone in our jail cell of hatred, we are stuck guarding the door. After the message a man introduced himself as a former prison inmate. He described how the guard at the gate of a prison is even more confined than a prisoner. The guard spends his day in a four-by-five-foot house. The prisoner has a ten-by-twelve cell. The guard can't leave; the prisoner gets to walk around. The prisoner can relax, but the guard has to be constantly alert. You might object and say, "Yes, but the guard of the prison gets to go home at night." True, but the guard of the prison of resentment doesn't.

If you're out to settle the score, you'll never rest. How can you? For one thing, your debtor may never pay. As much as you think you deserve an apology, your enemy may not agree. The racist may never repent. The chauvinist may never change. As justified as you are in your quest for vengeance, you may never get a penny's worth of justice. And if you do get some justice, will it be enough?

Let's really think about this one. How much justice is enough? Picture your enemy for a moment. Picture him tied to the whipping post. The strong-armed man with the whip turns to you and asks, "How many lashes?" And you give a number. The whip cracks, and the blood flows, and the punishment is inflicted. Your foe slumps to the ground, and you walk away.

Are you happy now? Do you feel better? Are you at peace? Perhaps for a while, but soon another memory will surface, and another lash will be needed, and . . . When does it all stop?

It stops when we start to forgive.

43.
IS IT OKAY FOR ME TO FIRE AN UNPRODUCTIVE WORKER? I'M A CHRISTIAN, BUT I'M ALSO A SUPERVISOR. HOW DO I SHOW LOVE TO A LAZY EMPLOYEE?

When we look at the love of Christ, we make a wonderful discovery. Love is more a decision than an emotion. You don't feel goose bumps and think sweet sentiments when you see your employee? Neither did Christ! In fact, there were times he felt everything but goose bumps. There was at least one time when he asked, "How long must I put up with you?" (Mark 9:19 NCV).

To love as Christ loved is not a matter of emotion but a matter of resolution to do whatever is in the best interest of the person.

This may mean applauding good behavior. Jesus applauded the faith of the centurion and the sacrifice of the woman with the alabaster bottle (Matt. 8:5–10; 26:6–13). Christlike love applauds good behavior.

At the same time, Christlike love refuses to endorse misbehavior. Jesus loved the woman who was caught in adultery, but he didn't dismiss her sin (John 8:2–11). Jesus loved his apostles, but he wasn't silent when they were faithless (Matt. 8:23–26). Jesus loved the people in the temple, but he didn't sit still when they were hypocritical (John 2:14–16). Love does whatever is in the best interest of a person.

The teenager says to his parents, "If you loved me, you'd let me come in as late as I want." That's a lie. Love does whatever is in the best interest of a person. Love sets curfews.

The cheating husband says to his wife, "If you loved me, you'd forget what has happened and let me come home." That may not be true. Love does what is in the best interest of a person. Love sets boundaries and seeks counsel.

The needy person says, "If the church loved me, it would pay all my bills." That may not be true. It might be more loving to provide a job for that person rather than give money to him.

The love of Christ is no sweet sentiment but rather a heartfelt resolve to do what is in the best interest of another person. Sometimes that means cleansing a temple. Other times that means dying on a cross.

44.
I'VE JUST DISCOVERED SOME THINGS ABOUT A FRIEND. HE'S BEEN MAKING MEAN COMMENTS ABOUT ME TO OTHERS. I'M TRYING TO FORGIVE HIM, BUT IT'S NOT EASY.

There was once a person in our world who brought Denalyn and me a lot of stress. She would call in the middle of the night. She was demanding and ruthless. She screamed at us in public. When she wanted something, she wanted it immediately, and she wanted it exclusively from us.

But we never asked her to leave us alone. We never told her to bug someone else. We never tried to get even.

After all, she was only a few months old.

It was easy for us to forgive our infant daughter's behavior because we knew she didn't know better.

Now, there is a world of difference between an innocent child and a deliberate destroyer. But there is still a point to my story: the way to handle a person's behavior is to understand the cause of it. One way to deal with people's peculiarities is to try to understand why they are peculiar.

Jesus knew Judas had been seduced by a powerful foe. He was aware of the wiles of Satan's whispers (he had just heard them himself). He knew how hard it was for Judas to do what was right.

He didn't justify what Judas did. He didn't minimize the deed. Nor did he release Judas from his choice. But he did look eye to eye at his betrayer and try to understand.

As long as you hate your enemy, a jail door is closed, and a prisoner is taken. But when you try to understand and release your foe from your hatred, then the prisoner is released, and that prisoner is you.

45. WHEN MY MOTHER'S HEALTH DETERIORATED, WE HAD TO PUT HER IN A NURSING HOME. MOM HAS ACCEPTED THE SITUATION, BUT I GET SO DEPRESSED ABOUT IT THAT I HAVE TO FORCE MYSELF TO VISIT HER. WHAT'S WRONG WITH ME?

For many years my mother was in an assisted-living facility not far from my house. The first few months I found it hard to see color amid the wrinkles, walkers, wheelchairs, and dentures. Each visit was a depressing reminder of my mom's failing health and fading memory.

Then I began to spot God's beauty among the people.

The loyalty of Elaine, also eighty-seven, who sat next to Mom at lunch. She cut my mother's food so she could eat it.

The unsquashable enthusiasm of Lois, nearly eighty, who, in spite of arthritis in both knees, volunteered to pour the morning coffee every day.

At first I saw age, disease, and faded vigor. With time I saw love, courage, and unflappable unselfishness.

Ask God to show you his work. He will be happy to do so.

46.

FOR THE PAST SIX MONTHS I'VE BEEN THE SOLE CARETAKER FOR MY MOM DURING MULTIPLE SURGERIES. THE EMOTIONAL AND PHYSICAL INTENSITY OF THIS LEAVES ME SO EXHAUSTED THAT I DON'T HAVE THE STRENGTH TO PRAY. DOES THIS MEAN THAT I AM DISAPPOINTING GOD OR THAT HE WON'T HELP ME IN THIS TRIAL?

We have an Advocate with the Father, Jesus Christ the righteous. (1 John 2:1 NKJV)

Do you know that you don't always have to be present in court? Sometimes your lawyer can speak for you. He understands these situations when you don't, and he speaks legalese while you stumble over the words.

You also have an advocate standing before the Father. When you are weak, he is strong. When you are timid, he speaks.

Jesus understands our every weakness. He lived in one of these tired, broken-down bodies! So he can stand in for us, appealing for us, when we just can't speak for ourselves.

We also have support from the Holy Spirit.

In the same way, the Spirit helps us in our weakness. We do not know what we ought to pray for, but the Spirit himself intercedes for us with groans that words cannot express. And he who searches our hearts knows the mind of the Spirit, because the Spirit intercedes for the saints in accordance with God's will. (Rom. 8:26–27)

Those sounds coming from your tired soul? Indecipherable? Hardly. The Holy Spirit speaks Groan-ese. Our groans are worth a thousand words.

"Uuuggghhh"—Help me, Lord. Get me out of this misery.

"Uhhhhhhhh"—I don't know what to do. The pain is too much.

"Ooohhhhhh"—Where is everyone?

God is not disappointed that we are so burdened we can't pray. He is sympathetic and picks up where we dropped off. With Jesus as your advocate and the Holy Spirit as your prayer partner, I bet you've been praying more than you think.

47.
I OFTEN WAKE UP IN THE MIDDLE OF THE NIGHT AND CAN'T GO BACK TO SLEEP. SO MUCH TO DO. SO MANY THINGS COULD GO WRONG. HOW CAN I CALM MY MIND?

The Greek word for *worry*, *merimnao*, stems from the verb *merizo* (divide) and *nous* (mind). Worry cleavers the mind, splitting thoughts between today and tomorrow. Today stands no chance against it. Fretting over tomorrow's problems siphons the strength you need for today, leaving you anemic and weak.

When you can't sleep, don't count sheep—read Scripture. Distinguish between God's voice and the voice of fear.

Worry takes a look at catastrophes and groans, "It's all coming unraveled."

God says, "Every detail in our lives of love for God is worked into something good" (Rom. 8:28 MSG).

Worry claims, "The world has gone crazy."

God's Word disagrees: "[Jesus has] done it all and done it well" (Mark 7:37 MSG).

Worry wonders if anyone is in control.

God's Word calls God "the blessed controller of all things" (1 Tim. 6:15 PHILLIPS).

Worry whispers this lie: "God doesn't know what I need."

God's Word declares, "God will take care of everything you need" (Phil. 4:19 MSG).

Worry never sleeps.

God's children do.

48. My anxiety is affecting my health, family, and work. Where do I turn?

I encourage you to share your fears with others. Pull back the curtains. Expose your fears, each and every one. Like vampires, they can't stand the sunlight. Financial fears, relationship fears, professional fears, safety fears—call them out in prayer. Drag them out by the hand of your mind, and make them stand before God and take their comeuppance!

Jesus made his fears public. He "offered up prayers and petitions with loud cries and tears to the one who could save him from death" (Heb. 5:7). He prayed loudly enough to be heard and recorded, and he begged his community of friends to pray with him.

His prayer in the Garden of Gethsemane becomes, for Christians, a picture of the church in action—a place where fears can be verbalized, pronounced, stripped down, and denounced; an escape from the wordless darkness of suppressed frights. A healthy church is where our fears go to die. We pierce them through with Scripture, psalms of celebration and lament. We melt them in the sunlight of confession. We extinguish them with the waterfall of worship, choosing to gaze at God, not our dreads.

Verbalize your angst to a trusted circle of God-seekers. The big deal (and good news) is this: you needn't live alone with your fear.

49.
My brother has been in a slump for weeks. He lost his job and, it seems, his motivation. What's going on?

The Bible talks about wilderness times. Your brother may be facing one. Jesus did.

Jesus was "in the wilderness for forty days, being tempted by the devil" (Luke 4:1–2 NASB). Jesus spent a month and ten days slugging it out with Satan. The wilderness is a long, lonely winter.

Doctor after doctor. Résumé after résumé. Diaper after diaper. Zoloft after Zoloft. Heartache after heartache. The calendar is stuck in February, and you're stuck in South Dakota, and you can't even remember what spring smells like.

In the wilderness you think the unthinkable. Jesus did. Wild possibilities crossed his mind. Teaming up with Satan? Opting to be a dictator and not a Savior? Torching Earth and starting over on Pluto? We don't know what he thought. We just know this: he was tempted. And "one is tempted when he is carried away and enticed by his own lust" (James 1:14 NASB). Temptation carries you and entices you. What was unimaginable prior to the wilderness becomes possible in it. A tough marriage can make a good man look twice at the wrong woman. Extended sickness makes even the stoutest soul consider suicide. Stress makes the smokiest nightclub smell sweet. In the wilderness you think the unthinkable.

For that reason the wilderness is the maternity ward for addictions. Binge eating, budget-busting gambling, excessive drinking, pornography—all short-term solutions to deep-seated problems. Typically they have no appeal, but in the wilderness you give thought to the unthinkable.

Urge your brother to rely on Scripture. Doubt doubts before doubting beliefs. Jesus told Satan, "Man shall not live on bread alone, but on every word that proceeds out of the mouth of God" (Matt. 4:4 NASB). The verb *proceeds* is literally "pouring out." Its tense suggests that God is constantly and aggressively communicating with the world through his Word. Wow! God is speaking still!

Your brother's time in the desert will pass. Jesus' did. "The devil left Him; and behold, angels came and began to minister to Him" (v. 11 NASB).

50.

I'VE TRIED TO BE A FRIEND TO A NEW KID IN OUR SCHOOL. HE'S FROM ANOTHER CULTURE, AND MOST OF THE KIDS IN SCHOOL TREAT HIM LIKE DIRT. NOW THEY'RE MAKING FUN OF ME FOR BEING FRIENDS WITH HIM. THIS REALLY HURTS, BUT I FEEL SORRY FOR HIM. I'M HIS ONLY FRIEND RIGHT NOW. WHAT SHOULD I DO?

Jews and Greeks were about as far apart as you could get on the philosophical/religious scale. Jews believed in one God, one truth, one Scripture. They pursued purity and righteousness. Greeks believed in many gods, many truths, and many writings of wisdom. They lived sensually—whatever felt good must be good.

The two groups rolled their eyes at each other. They despised each other. They never ate lunch together.

Along came Christianity and a man named Paul, who tried to reach out to both sides and reconcile them through his ministry.

For we were all baptized by one Spirit into one body—whether Jews or Greeks, slave or free—and we were all given the one Spirit to drink. (1 Cor. 12:13)

There is neither Jew nor Greek, slave nor free, male nor female, for you are all one in Christ Jesus. (Gal. 3:28)

Here there is no Greek or Jew, circumcised or uncircumcised, barbarian, Scythian, slave or free, but Christ is all, and is in all. (Col. 3:11)

The cause of prejudice is ignorance. People don't understand, so they attack and divide.

When we take away the skin color, the cultural garb, and the accent, we realize we are all the same.

We all want to be loved.

We all want to survive.

I would remain a friend to the new kid no matter what is said. The new kid is an unknown, but you are making him known. The first few jokes always sting, but over time the prejudice fades, the jokes get old, and people see that their mockery won't make a difference. Others look only at the surface and see differences. You obviously look deeper into this friend and see similarities.

Heaven is not divided into neighborhoods. Jews over here. Greeks here. Iranians over there. Peruvians in the middle. In fact, when the colors of heaven are mentioned, they are always expressed as a rainbow (Rev. 4:3; 10:1).

We should integrate ourselves with one another here on earth because it will be that way in heaven . . . where no one eats alone.

51. I'm a new Christian. Over the years I've developed a lot of bad habits. How do I get rid of them now?

By developing good ones. Here are four to start with:

First, the habit of prayer: "Base your happiness on your hope in Christ. When trials come endure them patiently; steadfastly maintain the *habit* of prayer" (Rom. 12:12 PHILLIPS, emphasis mine). Posture, tone, and place are personal matters. Select the form that works for you. But don't think about it too much. Better to pray awkwardly than not at all.

Second, the habit of study: "The man who looks into the perfect mirror of God's law . . . and makes a *habit* of so doing, is not the man who sees and forgets. He puts that law into practice and he wins true happiness" (James 1:25 PHILLIPS, emphasis mine).

Third, the habit of giving: "On *every Lord's Day* each of you should put aside something from what you have earned during the week, and use it for this offering. The amount depends on how much the Lord has helped you earn" (1 Cor. 16:2 TLB, emphasis mine). You don't give for God's sake. You give for your sake. "The purpose of tithing is to teach you always to put God first in your lives" (Deut. 14:23 TLB).

And last of all, the habit of fellowship: "Let us not give up the *habit* of meeting together, as some are doing. Instead, let us encourage one another" (Heb. 10:25 TEV, emphasis mine). You need support. You need what the Bible calls *fellowship.* And you need it every week.

Four habits worth having. Isn't it good to know that some habits are good for you?

52.
WHY DO WOMEN CHOOSE TO HAVE AN ABORTION? I JUST CAN'T UNDERSTAND HOW THEY CAN AGREE TO KILL THEIR UNBORN CHILD. THIS SEEMS SO BARBARIC.

It would be difficult to know and summarize every reason women choose to have an abortion, but I think most of the reasons can be found in a few areas.

Accidents happen: A woman sees the pregnancy as a mistake. This isn't the right time. This isn't the right father.

Clinical diagnosis: The fetus is described in medical terms, not human terms. They see the child as just cells, not as a human being.

Legal right: The law says we can, so we do. Since abortion is not penalized as murder, it must be acceptable.

Selfish priorities: The woman's (and/or man's) dreams and plans for the future do not include a child. The stronger survives.

Health concerns: The mother or the baby is diagnosed to have physical problems.

We can't overstate the difficulty of this decision. As a male, I do not pretend to understand the weight or the burden of an undesired pregnancy. At the same time we cannot overstate the inherent value of a human being and the sovereignty of God. Other than cases where abortion saves the life of the mother, we must protect the child.

And in all situations we must extend mercy. Many women who choose abortion are lost, scared, humiliated, guilt ridden, angry at themselves, alone. In some cases they were raped or violated. They don't need more condemnation, just clarification and compassion.

Look for ways to be a source of kindness. God is in the business of turning our mistakes into moments of grace.

53.
WHAT IF THE GLOBAL TEMPERATURE RISES A FEW MORE DEGREES? WHAT IF A TERRORIST GETS ON THE AIRPLANE I'M ON? WHAT IF THINGS ONLY GET WORSE IN THE WORLD? HOW DO I KEEP ALL THIS BAD NEWS IN PERSPECTIVE?

Paradise is not promised until Jesus returns. Peace, joy, and the absence of pain are promises of the future, not the present. Sin is still epidemic. But the cure is coming.

Remember that *Christ predicted the bad news.* Christ forewarned us about spiritual bailouts, ecological turmoil, and worldwide persecution. He told us things are going to get bad, really bad, before they get better. And when conditions worsen, "See to it that you are not alarmed" (Matt. 24:6). Jesus chose a stout term for *alarmed* that he used on no other occasion. It means "to wail, to cry aloud," as if Jesus counseled the disciples, "Don't freak out when bad stuff happens."

The only time we should get scared is when something surprises God. If something takes God by surprise, we are doomed. Since God knows all things, we are comforted.

If Christ can predict the problem, he can solve it. The same God who has the power of omniscience (knowing everything at every time) also has the power of omnipresence (being multipresent) and omnipotence (having all power). That trinitarian trifecta is unstoppable. All problems are too small in the shadow of God.

Take comfort; *it's the beginning of the end and the beginning of the new beginning.* In Matthew 24:8, Jesus called these challenges birth pangs. Birth pangs must occur before a new birth. During this time the mother keeps focused on the end result, the moment she gets to hold that beautiful baby in her arms. She knows birth pangs don't last forever and they signal a new beginning in her life. Calamities and catastrophes are the earthly pains that must occur before the birth of the new world. Hold on. Grit your teeth. The next push could be the last.

54.
WHEN PRAYERS AREN'T ANSWERED AND CALAMITIES HAPPEN, IS GOD SITTING ON HIS HANDS? WHY DOES GOD SOMETIMES OPT FOR SILENCE EVEN WHEN I'M SCREAMING MY LOUDEST?

Your question proposes two responses from God in difficult times:

God can not.

God will not.

Can God do anything when faced with disasters and calamities? The book of Daniel states: "[God] does as he pleases among the angels of heaven and among the people of the earth. No one can stop him or say to him, 'What do you mean by doing these things?'" (4:35 NLT).

The Bible declares clearly that God can. As Paul wrote, "God . . . is the blessed controller of all things, the king over all kings and the master of all masters" (1 Tim. 6:15 PHILLIPS).

Jesus can too. "The Son is . . . sustaining all things by his powerful word" (Heb. 1:3). God made it all. He holds the instruction manuals to everything. He knows how they work. God is unlimited in his power.

He can respond, and you can trust his strength.

Now, will God do anything when we need him to? Trickier question. I can't answer that. I would be God. That answer must trust his love and wisdom. God rescues those he wishes to rescue. He heals those he wants to heal. "I have tested you in the furnace of affliction. For My own sake, for My own sake, I will act" (Isa. 48:10–11 NASB).

He may respond, and you must trust his sovereignty.

Sometimes silence from God may be the best response. When you scream at God, do you really want him to scream back? Mountains shake before the Lord. When someone screams at me, I find the best response is silence. Peace begets peace. Anger stirs anger. Be glad God is silent at times like that.

Although God may not speak when we want him to, he is working, silently, behind the scenes, bringing the best possible solution to the situation.

So always remember:

God can get it done, and God's will *will* be done.

55. ON A DAILY BASIS WE'RE BOMBARDED WITH WORST-CASE-SCENARIO HEADLINES ABOUT ILLNESSES OR TERRORISM OR FINANCIAL COLLAPSE. THESE ARE VERY REAL CONCERNS. BUT WE CAN'T SPEND ALL DAY HIDING FROM LIFE. WHAT TYPE OF ADVICE WOULD YOU GIVE TO US?

Let's avoid the two extremes.

One extreme is the Chicken Little who runs around, saying, "The sky is falling, the sky is falling." That's called panic.

The other extreme is Pollyanna. Pollyanna is the one who says, "Oh, nothing bad is happening, nothing bad is happening. It's not bad. It's all good." That's called ignorance.

This world stinks sometimes. There's cancer and there's death in this world. There's sadness in this world. There are orphans in this world. There's hunger in this world. And sometimes you're going to pray for things, and the prayer isn't going to be answered the way you want. It's hard to be a Pollyanna when the sky is falling!

But somewhere between Chicken Little and Pollyanna are the sober, honest disciples of Christ who don't freak out at the presence of problems. Who don't lose faith when problems come. They know that all these problems are a natural unfolding of events.

For in the end, all believers will tumble skyward into the embrace of heaven, where nothing bad will ever happen again.

56. IF GOD CARES FOR HIS PEOPLE, WHY DO CHRISTIANS SUFFER PERSECUTION AND VIOLENCE? THIS SEEMS CONTRADICTORY.

I really want to find that verse in the Bible that promises no persecution and violence for Christians. I want to claim it and hold it up to God so Christians will never die for their faith again.

Unfortunately, I can't find it. I find just the opposite. Hebrews 11, the Bible's brief biography of God's best of the best, is difficult to read: "Others were tortured, not accepting deliverance, that they might obtain a better resurrection. Still others had trial of mockings and scourgings, yes, and of chains and imprisonment. They were stoned, they were sawn in two, were tempted, were slain with the sword. They wandered about in sheepskins and goatskins, being destitute, afflicted, tormented" (vv. 35–37 NKJV). This is how God treats his friends.

Jesus sent out the Twelve for an Israel-wide revival, promising healings and miracles for everyone—oh, and persecution. In Matthew 10, Jesus, in one of the most discouraging "Win One for the Gipper" speeches, said, "Be on your guard against men; they will hand you over to the local councils and flog you in their synagogues" (v. 17), "when they arrest you" (v. 19), "put [you] to death" (v. 21), "all men will hate you" (v. 22), "when you are persecuted" (v. 23), "do not be afraid of those who kill the body but cannot kill the soul" (v. 28). Thanks, Jesus. Can't wait.

Some of those friends liked persecution. Like Paul: "That is why, for Christ's sake, I delight in weaknesses, in insults, in hardships, in persecutions, in difficulties. For when I am weak, then I am strong" (2 Cor. 12:10). Paul thought it built character. Maybe he was right.

Persecution is inevitable. Even Jesus couldn't escape it. In fact, he became the poster child for persecution, the rallying cry of others who would die for their faith. Revelation speaks of martyred souls crying out for justice now and in the future (6:9–11).

Persecution is necessary for the advancement of the gospel. The death of Stephen in Acts 7 caused the gospel to spread to distant lands. Today in China, where persecution of Christians is high, the church is exploding in growth as those outside the faith see believers sacrificing their lives and their bodies.

But don't worry, persecution is not a problem.

Can anything separate us from the love Christ has for us? Can troubles or problems or sufferings or hunger or nakedness or danger or violent death? . . .

Nothing above us, nothing below us, nor anything else in the whole world will ever be able to separate us from the love of God that is in Christ Jesus our Lord. (Rom. 8:35, 39 NCV)

Sin is the problem, and we're here to help people overcome it even if it means risking our own lives.

57. Why is there so much chaos and evil in the world? It seems that no one cares about what God wants, and humanity is imploding.

Ever spin a top? The initial thrust forces it to spin powerfully, knocking over obstacles as it rips across the table. Then something starts to happen. The thrust weakens; the top wobbles. Now when it bounces off something, it teeters and totters. Finally the top is in a full-on death spin, until, boom . . . it crashes and stops.

That top is an example of the second law of thermodynamics, which explains why things, over time, slowly go from order to chaos.

The law is directly applied to the physical world of planets, baseballs, and tops, but indirectly it makes some sense in regard to the spiritual and moral fabric of our society.

As time goes on, things seem to spin more wildly out of control.

Sin caused the initial wobble in the garden. Ever since then the world has groaned for relief (Rom. 8:22). But is there a slow decline?

Jesus certainly warned us in Matthew 24 of wars, persecutions, and earthquakes, but many of those things have happened and still happen.

People all throughout time have thought that evil was running rampant:

~ the Roman persecution
~ the crusades
~ Hitler and World War II
~ Middle East terrorism

Sin works proportionately to the number of opportunities it is given. As communication and technology grow, sin expands with it. So while the world appears to be spinning out of control, it is only behaving as expected.

From our perspective, the world looks like chaos. From God's, it's all going according to schedule. From our perspective, evil is center stage. From God's, evil is taking a selfish bow during its final act.

58. I'M TROUBLED BY THE VESTIGES OF RACISM IN THE CHURCH. OUR CONGREGATION SEEMS OBLIVIOUS TO THE WHOLE TOPIC. IT'S NEVER MENTIONED. DIDN'T JESUS ADDRESS IT?

He certainly did.

He told the story of an affluent white man who was driving home from his downtown office. Since the hour was late and he was tired, he took the direct route, which led through the roughest part of the city. Wouldn't you know it—he ran out of gas. While walking to the convenience store, he was mugged and left for dead on the sidewalk.

A few minutes later a preacher drove by on the way to the evening church service. He saw the man on the sidewalk and started to help but then realized it would be too dangerous to stop.

Soon thereafter a respected seminary professor came by and saw the man but decided it was best not to get involved.

Finally, an old Hispanic immigrant driving a beat-up truck saw the man, stopped, and took him to the hospital. He paid the hospital bill and went on his way.

I altered the characters but not Jesus' question: "Which ... was a neighbor to the man?" (Luke 10:36). The answer? The man who responded with kindness. Neighborliness, then, is not defined by where you live but how you love. Your neighbor is not just the person in the next house but the one who needs your help. Your neighbor may be the person you've been taught not to love. For the Jew in the days of Jesus, it was a Samaritan.

For an Israeli today, it is a Palestinian.

For an Arab, a Jew.

For a black male, how about a pickup-driving, gun-toting, tobacco-chewing, baseball cap–wearing redneck?

For the Hispanic poor, how about the Hispanic affluent? For any Hispanic, how about the person who called you "wetback"?

For the white, the one who called you "gringo."

And for the black, the one who called you "boy."

Loving your neighbor is loving the person you used to hate.

A Christian has no excuse for prejudice. The prejudice of pagans can be explained, but in the case of a Christian, there is no explanation. No justification. We will never cross a cultural barrier greater than the one Jesus did. He learned our language, he lived in our world, he ate our food ... but most of all he took on our sins. How can we, who have been loved so much, not do the same for others? Those who find it hard to reach across racial differences should think twice. Unless they are Jews, a foreigner died on the cross for their sins.

59.

Does God allow war? If so, how do we reconcile his commands to love our enemies?

"Where do wars and fights come from among you? Do they not come from your desires for pleasure that war in your members?" (James 4:1 NKJV). War is the result of sin. To ask God to prohibit war, then, is to ask him to prohibit the consequence of human behavior. Something he has never been wont to do. As long as there is sin, there will be war.

In fact, God has used war to eradicate sin. When calling the Israelites into battle, Moses instructed them:

> After the LORD your God has done this for you, don't say in your hearts, "The LORD has given us this land because we are such good people!" No, it is because of the wickedness of the other nations that he is pushing them out of your way. (Deut. 9:4 NLT)

Can people grow so wicked, so pagan, so vile that God justifiably destroys them? Can leaders be so evil and cruel that God, knowing the hardness of their hearts, righteously removes them from the earth? Apparently so. He did so with Sodom and Gomorrah (Gen. 19:24–25). He did so with the Hittites, Amorites, Canaanites, Hivites, and Jebusites (Ex. 23:23).

> In those towns that the LORD your God is giving you as a special possession, destroy every living thing . . . This will prevent the people of the land from teaching you to imitate their detestable customs in the worship of their gods, which would cause you to sin deeply against the LORD your God. (Deut. 20:16, 18 NLT)

God has used warfare as a form of judgment against the enemies of God. In fact, he uses warfare as judgment against his own people when they become enemies of God.

God's priority is the salvation of souls. When a people group blockades his plan, does he not have the right to remove them? He is the God who knows "the end from the beginning" (Isa. 46:10). He knows the hearts of everyone and protects his people by punishing the evil of their wicked neighbors. Is it not God's right to punish evil? Is it not appropriate for the One who tells us to hate that which is evil to punish that which is evil? Of course it is.

I like the words of C. S. Lewis here:

Does loving your enemy mean not punishing him? No, for loving myself does not mean that I ought not to subject myself to punishment—even to death. If one had committed a murder, the right Christian thing to do would be to give yourself up to the police and be hanged. It is, therefore, in my opinion, perfectly right for a Christian judge to sentence a man to death or a Christian soldier to kill an enemy. I always have thought so, ever since I became a Christian and long before the war, and I still think so now that we are at peace. It is no good quoting "Thou shalt not kill." There are two Greek words: the ordinary word to *kill* and the word to *murder*. And when Christ quotes that commandment He uses the *murder* one in all three accounts, Matthew, Mark, and Luke. And I am told there is the same distinction in Hebrew. All killing is not murder any more than all sexual intercourse is adultery. When soldiers came to St. John the Baptist asking what to do, he never remotely suggested that they ought to leave the army: nor did Christ when He met a Roman sergeant-major—what they called a centurion. The idea of the knight—the Christian in arms for the defence of a good cause—is one of the great Christian ideas. War is a dreadful thing, and I can respect an honest pacifist, though I think he is entirely mistaken.[1]

60.

FRANKLY, I HAVE A HARD TIME CARING ABOUT PEOPLE IN OTHER CULTURES WHEN I HEAR ABOUT THE ATROCITIES THEY COMMIT AGAINST THEIR OWN PEOPLE OR EVEN AGAINST CHRISTIAN NATIONS. DOES GOD CARE MORE FOR ONE NATION OR CULTURE THAN ANOTHER?

Ever seen a tapestry? The finest artists weave together many colors and designs to create a beautiful palette. If it were just one color, it would be mistaken for a rag or a rug. But one look at this mosaic, and you want to put it someplace very special.

God loves the tapestry of nations. He loves Iraqis, Somalians, Israelis, New Zealanders, and Hondurans. He has a white-hot passion to harvest his children from every jungle, neighborhood, village, and slum. "*All the earth* shall be filled with the glory of the LORD" (Num. 14:21 ESV, emphasis mine). During the days of Joshua, God brought his people into Canaan "so that *all the peoples of the earth* may know that the hand of the LORD is mighty" (Josh. 4:24 ESV, emphasis mine). David commanded us to "sing to the LORD, *all the earth!* . . . Declare his glory among the nations, his marvelous works among *all the peoples!*" (Ps. 96:1, 3 ESV, emphasis mine). God spoke to us through Isaiah: "I will make you as a light for the nations, that my salvation may reach to the *end of the earth*" (Isa. 49:6 ESV, emphasis mine). His vision for the end of history includes "people for God from *every* tribe, language, people, and nation" (Rev. 5:9 NCV, emphasis mine).

God longs to proclaim his greatness in all 6,909 languages that exist in the world today.[2] He loves subcultures: the gypsies of Turkey, the hippies of California, the cowboys and rednecks of West Texas. He has a heart for bikers and hikers, tree huggers and academics. Single moms. Gray-flanneled executives. He loves all people groups and equips us to be his voice. He commissions common Galileans, Nebraskans, Brazilians, and Koreans to speak the languages of the peoples of the world. He teaches us the vocabulary of distant lands, the dialect of the discouraged neighbor, the vernacular of the lonely heart, and the idiom of the young student. God outfits his followers to cross cultures and touch hearts.

Jesus himself traveled to the forgotten in Bethlehem, the foreigners in Egypt, the laughable no-gooders in Nazareth, the eccentric in Jerusalem, the half-breed Samaritans, and the pig-eating, idol-worshipping Gerasenes (Matt. 2:1; 2:13–23; 20:17; John 4:5; Matt. 8:28). His mission field was the lost sheep of Israel, but he could not help but take his healing and hope to whomever would respond.

And before he left, Jesus commissioned his followers (that includes us) to go to the whole world . . . all of it . . . every nook and cranny of every nation . . . to bring a stop to the exact atrocities you speak of and hope to those struggling in oppression.

Every believer from every nation brings out the color and diversity of the tapestry of heaven.

Help

Prayer, Scripture,
and "Why church?"

Kevin,

Knowing God is like mountain-climbing. Some days the path is steep. Others, the trail is easy. Clouds can eclipse the view. The sun might illuminate the peak. Most of all, it just takes time.

Know This: God will help you.

Max

61.
WHY SHOULD WE PRAY FOR HELP WHEN GOD ALREADY HAS A PLAN? HE'S GOING TO DO HIS WILL ANYWAY, SO WHAT DIFFERENCE DOES IT MAKE WHEN WE ASK FOR HEALING FOR A FRIEND, FAMILY MEMBER, OR PET? DOES PRAYER REALLY CHANGE ANYTHING, OR WAS THE OUTCOME ALREADY IN GOD'S PLAN?

I have a story that helps answer this question.

When my daughter Sara was in the second grade, we took her desk hunting at a store that specializes in unpainted furniture. She was excited about owning her own desk. When she learned we weren't taking the desk home that day, she was upset. "But, Daddy, I wanted to take it home today."

Much to her credit, she didn't stomp her feet and demand her way. She did, however, set out on an urgent course to change her father's mind. Every time I turned a corner, she was waiting for me.

"Daddy, don't you think we could paint it ourselves?"

"Daddy, I just want to draw some pictures on my new desk."

"Daddy, please let's take it home today."

After a bit she disappeared, only to return, arms open wide, bubbling with a discovery. "Guess what, Daddy. It'll fit in the back of the car!"

You and I know that a seven-year-old has no clue what will or won't fit in a vehicle, but the fact that she had measured the trunk with her arms softened my heart. The clincher, though, was the name she called me: Daddy.

The Lucado family took a desk home that day.

She changed my mind. She altered my schedule. She influenced the details of my actions.

Prayer does the same.

Remember the prayer of Moses on Mount Sinai? He begged God not to destroy the people, and "the LORD changed his mind and did not destroy the people as he had said he might" (Ex. 32:14 NCV).

The prayer of Moses affected the plans of God.

Prayer does not change everything. We cannot convince God to stop loving people, preparing heaven, or saving souls. We cannot change God's character or his eternal plans.

But we can influence the details. "When a believing person prays, great things happen" (James 5:16 NCV). Prayer is not overcoming a reluctant God. Prayer is urging God to do what he wants to do (heal, help, give his daughter a desk) but to do it sooner, stronger, or more clearly.

By the way, I ordered a desk for my office that day too. When Sara learned that it would take six weeks to be delivered, she told me, "I guess you didn't beg, did you, Daddy?"

62.

I'M A NEW CHRISTIAN WHO IS TRYING TO FIGURE OUT HOW TO GROW CLOSER TO GOD. FRIENDS TELL ME I NEED TO HAVE A QUIET TIME WITH GOD EACH DAY, BUT I CAN'T FIGURE OUT EXACTLY WHAT TO DO.

Denalyn and I like to go to the same restaurants over and over again. You could call our dates predictable, but for us they are special. We like the food. We like the servers. We like the atmosphere. When we're there, we remember special moments we've shared before. Our hearts open up . . . we lose track of time . . . because we're comfortable in that place. We talk to each other, listen to each other, laugh, and cry. I love those times!

A quiet time with God is very similar to a date. Here are some tools to help you keep your very special date with God.

Decide on *a regular time and place.* Select a slot in your schedule and a corner of your world, and claim it for God. A familiar place will remind you of similar feelings you experienced before with God. You need to get comfortable.

How much time should you take? As much as you need. Value quality over quantity. Your time with God should last long enough for you to say what you want and for God to say what he wants.

You should bring on your date *an open Bible*—God's Word, his love letter to you. You won't necessarily hear God speak out loud, but you can hear what he has to say through his eternal dialogue with humanity.

You also need *a listening heart.* Don't forget the admonition from James: "The man who looks into the perfect mirror of God's law, the law of liberty, and makes a habit of so doing, is not the man who sees and forgets. He puts that law into practice and he wins true happiness" (James 1:25 PHILLIPS). Listen to the lover of your soul. Don't just nod your head, pretending to hear. Your date knows when you're engaged. So does God.

Just as you wouldn't miss your date with a loved one, claiming you were too busy, make sure your date with God is on the calendar, and do everything in your power to keep it special.

63.

I'M REALLY STRUGGLING THROUGH SOME TOUGH TIMES RIGHT NOW, BOTH FINANCIALLY AND PERSONALLY. I DON'T SEEM TO HAVE THE ANSWERS OR SOLUTIONS. CAN PRAYER REALLY HELP ME FIND ANSWERS AND GET THROUGH THIS SLUMP?

Prayer reminds you who is in charge. You don't take your requests to someone with less authority. You take them to someone who outranks you in the solutions department. Prayer decreases you and increases God.

Prayer gives permission to God to complete the request according to his will. Hopefully, you don't pray just to let God know what's going on. He's way ahead of you on that one. You are praying to transfer "my will be done" to "God's will be done." Since he is in charge, he knows the best solution. Prayer exercises your willpower and gives God authority to work in your life.

Prayer relieves the stress of perceived inactivity. Now that God has been given the task, you don't have to worry about it any longer. God has his people on it. With less stress comes more strength. Prayer transfers the burden to God and lightens your load.

People struggle with life when they don't have answers. The darkest valleys are blackened by the shadows of question marks. So what do you do? Think harder? Try harder? Hold longer conversations with yourself? Why not pray to the One with all the answers and let him take over?

Prayer pushes us through life's slumps, propels us over the humps, and pulls us out of the dumps. Prayer is the oomph we need to get the answers we seek.

64.

I'VE ASKED GOD TO HEAL ME FROM CANCER. HE HEALED MY
FRIEND FROM CANCER, BUT SO FAR HE HASN'T HELPED ME. MY
FRIEND SAYS I SHOULD PRAY WITH MORE FAITH. IS SHE RIGHT?

Let me share with you two false notions people have about heavenly healing.

First, *death is always bad*. We see a hearse; we think sorrow. We see a grave; we think despair. We hear of a death; we think of a loss. Not so in heaven. When heaven sees the breathless body, it sees the vacated cocoon and the liberated butterfly. Ever since sin entered the world, the body has been doomed to die. Not only is death inevitable; death is necessary for us to inherit the new life we are to enjoy in Christ. "Flesh and blood cannot have a part in the kingdom of God . . . This body that can be destroyed must clothe itself with something that can never be destroyed" (1 Cor. 15:50, 53 NCV).

As long as we see death as a failure, then we will perceive God as being deaf to our prayers. Ask those in heaven if their prayers for healing were answered, and you might get a different perspective.

Second, *prayer heals*. God heals, not prayer. A matter of semantics? No. If you think the power is in the prayer and not the One who hears the prayer, you fault the pray-er for unanswered prayer. How many people have had to deal with the false guilt of inadequate prayer? "If I had prayed more, if I had prayed better, if I had prayed differently, if I had prayed in the chapel or with a priest or with rosary beads or with different words." To claim that prayer heals is to place prayer in the realm of magic chants and medicine man dances. Worse still, to place the power in the prayer relegates God to the personality of a computer. If I push the right buttons or type the correct code, he must respond.

No, the power of prayer is in the One who hears it, not the one who makes it.

Don't assume that the faithful will never suffer. If the faithful never suffer, how do we explain the illness of Paul (Gal. 4:13), the poor health of Paul's friend Trophimus (2 Tim. 4:20), and the near death of his beloved Epaphroditus (Phil. 2:27)?

Hebrews 11 describes the plight of God's faithful: some defeated kingdoms, stopped fires, and were saved from being killed. Others were put in chains and thrown into prison. They were stoned to death, they were cut in half, and they were killed with swords. Some wore the skin of sheep and goats. They were poor, abused, and treated badly . . . All of these people are known for their faith (Heb. 11:33–39).

If the faithful never suffer, how do we explain the agony of Gethsemane and the death of Christ on the cross? Jesus, himself, prayed to be delivered from earthly pain (Matt. 26:39), and that request was denied. Was that due to a lack of faith? Absolutely not. God said no to the earthly prayer for a heavenly reason. The plan of salvation was worth the pain of the Savior. There are times when God chooses to say no to the earthly request so he can say yes to the heavenly one.

Doesn't he still do that today? Doesn't he use the challenge of the body to strengthen the soul? We need to remember that Peter was in a storm before he walked on water, Lazarus was in a grave before he came out of it, the demoniac was possessed before he was a preacher, and the paralytic was on a stretcher before he was in your Bible (Matt. 14:23–29; John 11:1–44; Mark 5:1–20; Luke 5:17–25). We know that in everything God works for the good of those who love him (Rom. 8:28).

Please don't interpret the presence of your disease as the absence of God's love. I pray he heals you. And he will, ultimately.

65.

I'VE READ THE VERSE IN THE BIBLE ABOUT PRAYING WITHOUT CEASING. DOES ANYONE ACTUALLY DO THIS?

Unceasing prayer may sound complicated, but it needn't be that way.

Do this. Change your definition of prayer. Think of prayers less as an activity for God and more as an awareness of God. Seek to live in uninterrupted awareness. Acknowledge his presence everywhere you go. As you stand in line to register your car, think, *Thank you, Lord, for being here.* In the grocery store as you shop, think, *Your presence, my King, I welcome.* As you wash the dishes, worship your Maker. Brother Lawrence did. This well-known saint called himself the "lord of all pots and pans." In his book *The Practice of the Presence of God,* he wrote:

> The time of business does not with me differ from the time of prayer; and in the noise and clatter of my kitchen, while several persons are at the same time calling for different things, I possess God in as great tranquillity as if I were upon my knees at the blessed sacrament.[1]

Besides, it makes more sense to talk to God than mumble to yourself.

66.
I APPLIED FOR A JOB AND GOT REJECTED. I ASKED MY
GRANDMOTHER FOR A LOAN; SHE TURNED ME DOWN. MY
BOYFRIEND SAYS WE SHOULD SPLIT UP. I'M HAVING A HARD, HARD WEEK. IS
GOD EVEN LISTENING TO ME?

Yes, he is. And here is what you need to know: God knows more about life than we do.

When my oldest daughter was about six years old, she and I were having a discussion about my work. It seems she wasn't too happy with my chosen profession. She wanted me to leave the ministry. "I like you as a preacher," she explained. "I just really wish you sold snow cones."

An honest request from a pure heart. It made sense to her that the happiest people in the world were the men who drove the snow-cone trucks. You play music. You sell goodies. You make kids happy. What more could you want? (Come to think about it, she may have had a point. I could get a loan, buy a truck, and . . . nah, I'd eat too much.)

I heard her request but didn't heed it. Why? Because I knew better. I know what I'm called to do and what I need to do. The fact is, I knew more about life than she did. Same with God.

God hears our requests. But his answer is not always what we'd like it to be. Why? Because God knows more about life than we do.

Next time you're disappointed, don't panic. Don't bail out. Don't give up. Just be patient. Talk to God about your challenges. Then let your heavenly Father remind you he's still in control.

67. IN MY MED-SCHOOL CLASS WE DISCUSSED THE PLACE OF PRAYER IN THE HOSPITAL. AS YOU CAN IMAGINE, WE HEARD STRONG OPINIONS ON BOTH SIDES. WHAT ARE YOUR THOUGHTS? WHAT IS THE PURPOSE OF HEALING PRAYER?

We tend toward one of two extremes on this subject: fanaticism or cynicism. Fanatics see the healing of the body as the aim of God and the measure of faith. Cynics consider any connection between prayer and healing as coincidental at best and misleading at worst. A fanatic might seek prayer at the exclusion of medicine; a cynic might seek medicine at the exclusion of prayer.

A healthy balance can be found. The physician is the friend of God. Prayer is the friend of the physician.

The example of Jesus is important.

Great crowds came to Jesus, bringing with them the lame, the blind, the crippled, those who could not speak, and many others. They put them at Jesus' feet, and he healed them. The crowd was amazed when they saw that people who could not speak before were now able to speak. The crippled were made strong. The lame could walk, and the blind could see. And they praised the God of Israel for this. (Matt. 15:30–31 NCV)

What did the people do with the sick? They put them at Jesus' feet. This is the purpose of praying for the ill. We place the sick at the feet of the Physician and request his touch. This passage also gives us the result of healing prayer. "They praised the God of Israel for this." The ultimate aim of healing is not just a healthy body but a greater kingdom. If God's aim is to grant perfect health to all his children, he has failed, because no one enjoys perfect health, and everyone dies. But if God's aim is to expand the boundaries of his kingdom, then he has succeeded. For every time he heals, a thousand sermons are preached.

Speaking of sermons, did you notice what is missing from this text? Preaching. Jesus stayed with these four thousand people for three days and, as far as we know, never preached a sermon. Not one time did he say, "May I have your attention?" But thousands of times he asked, "May I help you?" What compassion he had for them. Can you imagine the line of people? On crutches, wearing blindfolds, carried by friends, cradled by parents. For seventy-two hours Jesus stared into face after hurting face, and then he said, "I feel sorry for these people" (v. 32 NCV). The inexhaustible compassion of Jesus. Mark it down. Pain on earth causes pain in heaven. And he will stand and receive the ill as long as the ill come in faith to him.

And he will do what is right every time. "God will always give what is right to his people who cry to him night and day, and he will not be slow to answer them" (Luke 18:7 NCV).

Healing prayer begs God to do what is right. My friend Dennis, a chaplain, offers this prayer over patients: "God, would you put on the surgical gloves first?"

I like that.

68. If God doesn't tempt us, why does he tell us to pray, "Lead us not into temptation"?

Because of the translation, many think this statement is saying, "Don't tempt me, Lord" or "Don't lead me into a sin." That's not the intent. God is not tempting us or leading us into temptation. The phrase translates better as a cry for help: "Keep me from falling into a temptation trap."

We are asking God to steer us away from the bar, to divert our attention when the pretty girl walks by, to give us wisdom when we find that wallet, to walk away when we find ourselves alone with someone else's spouse.

The Father loves to hold the hands of his children. "The Lord directs the steps of the godly. He delights in every detail of their lives. Though they stumble, they will never fall, for the Lord holds them by the hand" (Ps. 37:23–24 NLT).

Temptation comes from only one place—hell. Satan has tempted everyone, starting with Adam and including even Jesus. The first with fruit. The second with bread. God does not tempt. He does not set us up to fail.

God does test us. Job was not tempted by God. His faith was tested. Satan (and Job's wife and friends) tempted Job to curse God (Job 1:8–12; 2:9; 42:7). Peter's faith was tested by walking on water (Matt. 14:25–31). Peter was tempted when he told Jesus not to have such morbid thoughts about death. Jesus blasted back, "Get out of here, Satan" (see Matt. 16:21–23).

So our prayers ask God, as the ultimate path guide, to watch the road ahead and warn us of places where we might stumble.

69. Our son (sixteen years old) was diagnosed with a mental illness three years ago. We have prayed without ceasing for God's healing. But healing has not come, and the atmosphere in our home is becoming increasingly tense. Should we keep praying for his healing or just accept that he will never be healed?

It's always right to pray. Scripture tells us of many parents who pleaded with God for their children. Your son is just as important to God as those children of long ago.

If you will bear with me for a moment, let's come at this from a different perspective. I find it fascinating that the thread count of bedsheets can be anywhere between eighty and fifteen hundred threads per square inch of fabric. The higher the count, the better quality the sheet. Hundreds of threads woven in and out, over and under, to create one fabric.

I think about the nearly seven billion threads of life woven in and out of each other that create this tapestry on earth.[2] All of them placed here by the Creator, holding each other together.

Your son is one of those threads. His life wraps around the lives of others, holding them together as they hold him together, woven there by God himself. We may think it's a weak thread that needs to be fixed, but God may see it as the strongest thread around.

Maybe your son's illness is the thread that keeps you focused on God. Maybe your son's illness is the key to a neighbor coming to accept Christ. Maybe your son's illness becomes a testimony that blesses people for years to come. We have no idea how our lives weave in and out of the work God is doing in others.

So can your son be healed? Yes. Jesus healed mental illness in Bible times (Luke 9:37–42), and since God never changes, he can heal your son today.

Will your son be healed? We cannot say. It's not your decision or mine or even your son's. It's the decision of the Weaver. We see only one thread, but God sees them all.

The real healing that needs to occur, and a major issue that you seem to be facing, is the tension in the house. Relationships are pulling apart. Your family's faith is hanging by a thread.

God can bring that healing to your family now if they will come to him with their tired, worn-out lives and ask for a new wardrobe. Pray for healing, but pray for more than just physical healing.

70.

IT IS EMBARRASSING FOR ME TO ADMIT THIS, BUT IT'S A STRUGGLE FOR ME TO PRAY. I WANT TO PRAY MORE, BUT IT SEEMS AS THOUGH I CAN'T PRAY FOR MORE THAN A FEW MINUTES WITHOUT GETTING DISTRACTED. WHY DOES THIS HAPPEN TO ME? DOES IT MEAN I'M A WEAK CHRISTIAN?

When we pray, Satan plays games with us.

His favorite is spin the mind. Keep the thoughts circling round and round in an unfocused maelstrom of activity so the person praying believes he is too busy to finish.

Then Satan pulls out pin the blame on the donkey. That's when prayer time turns into the blame game. Instead of praying for people, we start accusing them. "If only they would do this . . ." or "God, tell them to do that . . ." Instead of confessing our sin, we load our burdens on the pack mules of our lives.

Usually Satan finishes with a game of lost-and-seek, where we get lost in our thoughts, wandering down empty trails and chasing shadows, then try to find our way back, only to discover the game is over.

Praying isn't a game. In fact, it's serious business—so serious that Satan plays games with our minds to keep us from praying.

Why? Because God tells us to "pray without ceasing" (1 Thess. 5:17 NKJV). He sees church as "a house of prayer" (Matt. 21:13). No other activity guarantees such results: "When two of you get together on anything at all on earth and make a prayer of it, my Father in heaven goes into action" (Matt. 18:19 MSG). When people pray, things happen. "The effective, fervent prayer of a righteous man avails much" (James 5:16 NKJV).

If Satan can stop prayer, he can make Christians ineffective.

The best way to stay focused is to remember the purpose of praying. Give each of these parts of your prayer outline ample time—five to ten minutes. They spell the acronym ACTS.

Adoration—Give God praise.

Confession—Confess your sins (not other people's sins).

Thanksgiving—Show appreciation for all God has given you.

Supplication—Present prayer requests for yourself and others.

No wonder Satan wants to convince us that we are weak, because once a believer finds strength in prayer, the game is over for Satan.

71. IT'S NOT HARD FOR ME TO TRUST GOD TO ANSWER EVERYDAY PRAYERS AND REQUESTS, BUT WHEN A REALLY IMPOSSIBLE SITUATION COMES INTO MY LIFE, MY FAITH IN GOD'S POWER SEEMS TO GO OUT THE WINDOW. HOW CAN I INCREASE MY FAITH THAT MY PRAYERS WILL BE ANSWERED?

Check his résumé.

You want to know his power? Take a look at his creation. Curious about his strength? Pay a visit to his home address: 1 Billion Starry Sky Avenue. Want to know his size? Step out into the night, and stare at starlight emitted one million years ago, and then read 2 Chronicles 2:6: "No one can really build a house for our God. Not even the highest of heavens can hold him" (NCV).

He is untainted by the atmosphere of sin, unbridled by the time line of history, unhindered by the weariness of the body.

What controls you doesn't control him. What troubles you doesn't trouble him. What fatigues you doesn't fatigue him. Is an eagle disturbed by traffic? No, he rises above it. Is the whale perturbed by a hurricane? Of course not. He plunges beneath it. Is the lion flustered by the mouse standing directly in his way? No, he steps over it.

How much more is God able to soar above, plunge beneath, and step over the troubles of the earth! "With God all things are possible" (Matt. 19:26 NKJV). Our questions betray our lack of understanding:

How can God be everywhere at one time? (Who says God is bound by a body?)

How can God hear all the prayers that come to him? (Perhaps his ears are different from ours.)

How can God be the Father, the Son, and the Holy Spirit? (Could it be that heaven has a different set of physics than earth?)

If people down here won't forgive me, how much more guilty am I before a holy God? (Oh, just the opposite. God is always able to give grace when we humans can't—he invented it.)

How vital that we pray, armed with the knowledge that God is in heaven. Pray with any lesser conviction, and your prayers are timid, shallow, and hollow. But spend some time walking in the workshop of the heavens, seeing what God has done, and watch how your prayers are energized.

72.

CAN WE BELIEVE THE BIBLE? HOW CAN WE KNOW IT IS ANYTHING MORE THAN A COLLECTION OF SAYINGS AND STORIES? CAN WE TRULY BELIEVE THAT THE BIBLE IS THE WORD OF GOD?

There are many reasons I believe in the Bible. Here are a few:

Composition. It was composed over sixteen centuries by forty authors with one central theme. Written by soldiers, shepherds, scholars, and fishermen. Begun by Moses in lonely Arabia, finished by John on lonely Patmos. Penned by kings in palaces, shepherds in tents, and inmates in prisons.

Forty writers, most unknown to each other, writing in different countries and three different languages, separated by three times the number of centuries since Columbus discovered America—was it possible for these authors to produce a book of singular theme unless behind them there was one mind, one designer? The Bible is remarkable in composition.

Durability. It is the single most published book in history. The top seller for three hundred years. Translated into twelve hundred languages by an army of translators. Bibles have been burned by dictators and banished from courtrooms, but God's Word continues. The death knell has tolled a hundred times, but each time the grave is opened, and God's Word continues. The Bible is remarkable in durability.

Prophecy. The pages of your Bible contain more than three hundred fulfilled prophecies about the life of Christ. A substantial biography was written about Jesus five hundred years before he was born. Can you imagine if the same occurred today? Can you imagine if we found a book written in 1900 that prophesied two world wars, a depression, an atomic bomb, and the assassinations of John F. Kennedy and Martin Luther King? What would we think of the book? Wouldn't we trust it?

Applicability. Paul says the Bible "is useful for teaching, for showing people what is wrong in their lives, for correcting faults, and for teaching how to live right" (2 Tim. 3:16 NCV).

Apply the principles of stewardship to your budget, and see if you don't get out of debt.

Apply the principles of fidelity to your marriage, and see if you don't have a happier home.

Apply the principles of forgiveness to your relationships, and see if you aren't more peaceful.

Apply the principles of honesty at school, and see if you don't succeed.

Apply the Bible, and see if you don't agree—the Bible works.

73.
JESUS WASHED HIS DISCIPLES' FEET. SHOULD WE? PAUL COMMANDED THE WOMEN IN CORINTH TO WEAR VEILS ON THEIR HEADS. WHY DON'T WE DO SO TODAY? HE COMMANDED THE CHRISTIANS IN ROME TO GREET ONE ANOTHER WITH A HOLY KISS. ARE WE DISOBEYING IF WE DON'T PUCKER UP? I GUESS I'M WONDERING, HOW DO WE KNOW WHAT IS A COMMAND AND WHAT IS CULTURAL?

The Bible is God's Word given in humanity's language.

It was written in another time.

It was written in another culture.

It was written in another language.

Scripture marries eternal truth with historical particularity. How do we separate the two?

We ask the basic question of Bible interpretation: "What is its purpose?"

Some believe the Bible provides the student with a secret code of prophecy that, once deciphered, will reveal the day on which our Lord will return. Others believe the Bible is a secret success manual for wealth and health. Still others use the Bible to substantiate already-held beliefs. Some Christians feel the purpose of the Bible is to provide a pattern for the organization of the New Testament church.

Though the Bible comments on each of these subjects, none of them identifies the purpose of Scripture. What is the purpose of the Bible? Let the Bible itself answer that question.

Since you were a child you have known the Holy Scriptures which are able to make you wise. And that wisdom leads to salvation through faith in Christ Jesus. (2 Tim. 3:15 NCV)

These are written that you may believe that Jesus is the Christ, the Son of God, and that by believing you may have life in his name. (John 20:31)

I am not ashamed of this Good News about Christ. It is God's powerful method of bringing all who believe it to heaven. This message was preached first to the Jews alone, but now everyone is invited to come to God in this same way. This Good News tells us that God makes us ready for heaven—makes us right in God's sight—when we put our faith and trust in Christ to save us. (Rom. 1:16–17 TLB)

The purpose of the Bible is simply to proclaim God's plan to save his children. It asserts that people are lost and need to be saved. And it communicates the message that Jesus is God in the flesh, sent to save his children.

The purpose of the Bible is not to transplant an ancient culture into our generation but to reveal the gospel to it.

Still, the first-century practices of footwashing, a holy kiss, and veil-wearing are helpful. Let's learn from the principle behind each one. Footwashing teaches humility. The holy kiss models hospitality. Veil-wearing exemplifies respect for culture. We imitate the principle, not the particular practice.

Remember: the big message of the Bible is God's plan to populate his new kingdom. Everything else is secondary.

74. Can we be sure that the text of the Bible we read is exactly what God wanted to write? With so many years between Bible times and our day, isn't it possible that his words and thoughts could have been changed by the writers?

All Scripture is God-breathed and is useful for teaching, rebuking, correcting and training in righteousness, so that the man of God may be thoroughly equipped for every good work. (2 Tim. 3:16–17)

The Bible makes a statement about itself. A bold statement.

"I am God-breathed."

This self-declaration says the words found in its pages have come from God's heart and were pushed out of his mouth and into the world. Where did those words go? To the ears and hearts of scribes, kings, and prophets, who took notes, then passed them on to us.

But were they accurate notes?

Some books were transcribed a thousand years after they happened (Genesis), while some were published twenty to thirty years after the events (the Gospels). Some were recorded by people who weren't there (some believe Samuel wrote Judges); others saw it all firsthand (Luke traveled with Paul and wrote Acts).

As for the content, did words change over time? Were there mistakes in the copies of the copies of the copies?

Maybe. Probably. Some minor word-order variations. A misspelling crept in now and then. These things happen when humans breathe on anything—literary hiccups, burps, and coughs.

God knew that when he breathed the Bible into people, they could potentially make huge mistakes, so he employed the Holy Spirit to guide those words to us today—inspiring, reminding, awakening, clarifying.

The God who had the power to make those incidents happen long ago has the power to get his holy words through wars, memory loss, and persecutions.

We must believe that the Bible in our hands is the Bible that God wanted us to have.

75.

I'VE READ IN THE BIBLE ABOUT BEING FILLED WITH GOD'S SPIRIT, BUT I'M NOT SURE WHAT THIS MEANS. CAN CHRISTIANS HAVE DIFFERENT AMOUNTS OF THE SPIRIT IN THEIR LIVES AT DIFFERENT TIMES? WHAT DO I NEED TO DO TO HAVE MORE OF THE SPIRIT IN MY LIFE?

In a car, gas powers a combustible engine. The more I drive, the more gas gets used. When I'm running near empty, I race to the gas station and fill up with more.

Paul, in Ephesians 5:18, is the spiritual Chevron man and gives us this piece of advice for our spiritual engines: "Fill 'er up with the Holy Spirit."

I addressed this question in my book *Come Thirsty*:

> Not only does Paul give a command; he gives a continuous, collective command. Continuous in the sense that the filling is a daily privilege. Collective because the invitation is offered to all people. "You *all* be filled with the Spirit." Young, old, servants, businessmen, seasoned saints, and new converts. The Spirit will fill all. No SAT (Spiritual Aptitude Test) required. You don't need to persuade him to enter; he already has. Better set another plate for dinner. You've got company. "Your body is a temple for the Holy Spirit who is in you" (1 Cor. 6:19 NCV). As a Christian, you have all the power you need for all the problems you face.

You don't have to race to church or a local conference to get filled—though the Holy Spirit has pumps there. He also has stations in your home, at your school, at work—wherever you are—because that's where he is.

You may run out of patience or reach the limits of your strength, but you haven't run out of access to the Holy Spirit. Since he lives in all believers, we all carry the entire gas station with us everywhere we go. God's Holy Spirit can flow into your life like oil through the Alaskan pipeline—crude, raw, unfiltered power, gushing down from the thrones of heaven and pouring into your heart.

However, merely being at the gas station doesn't fill your tank. It takes some effort. You have to flip the switch. You have to want more Spirit.

The Holy Spirit also isn't a tangible commodity that can be measured from full to empty on life's dashboard. It doesn't run out in that sense. Our sense of fullness is better compared to a relationship than a tank. The more focus and time I put into a relationship, the more full, the more connected, I feel.

Through prayer, Bible study, meditation, serving, and journaling, you connect with God and fill your tank, each time saying you want more of God's Spirit. As a result, you feel filled, maybe even to overflowing!

He'll power as much as you give him—your schedule, your time, your dreams, your today, your tomorrow, your thoughts, your prayers.

So start the pumps. Let the Holy Spirit flow into your entire life. All who are ready . . . fill 'er up.

> Everyone who asks will receive . . . You know how to give good things to your children. How much more your heavenly Father will give the Holy Spirit to those who ask him! (Luke 11:10, 13 NCV)

76. I believe that God's Holy Spirit is here on earth to help believers. But exactly how does it function in the life of a believer?

The Holy Spirit is not an it. He is a person. He has knowledge (1 Cor. 2:11). He has a will (1 Cor. 12:11). He has a mind (Rom. 8:27). He has affections (Rom. 15:30). You can lie to him (Acts 5:3–4). You can insult him (Heb. 10:29). You can grieve him (Eph. 4:30).

The Holy Spirit is not an impersonal force. He is not Popeye's spinach or the surfer's wave. He is God within you to help you. In fact, John calls him the Helper.

Here's a word picture to use. Envision a father helping his son learn to ride a bicycle. The father stays at the son's side. He pushes the bike and steadies it if the boy starts to tumble. The Spirit does the same for us; he stays our step and strengthens our stride. Unlike the earthly father who eventually releases his grip on the bike and allows his son to journey down the road on his own, the Holy Spirit never leaves. He is with us to the end of the age.

What does he look like? "God is Spirit, and those who worship Him must worship in spirit and truth" (John 4:24 NKJV). Since the Holy Spirit is spirit, he is invisible, unseen by the human eye. But that doesn't mean his work is unseen or unfelt.

He comforts the saved. "When I go away, I will send the Helper to you" (John 16:7 NCV).

He convicts the lost. "When the Helper comes, he will prove to the people of the world the truth about sin, about being right with God, and about judgment" (John 16:8 NCV).

He conveys the truth. "I have many more things to say to you, but they are too much for you now. But when the Spirit of truth comes, he will lead you into all truth" (John 16:12–13 NCV).

So think about it. Have you ever been comforted? Has God ever brought you peace when the world brought you pain?

Have you ever been convicted? Have you ever sensed a stab of sorrow for your actions?

Have you ever understood a new truth? Or seen an old principle in a new way? The light comes on. Your eyes pop open. "Aha, now I understand." Ever happen to you?

If so, then the Holy Spirit has been working inside you.

Finally, the Holy Spirit is the heartbeat of the believer. He is the resurrection power that raised Jesus. "And if the Spirit of him who raised Jesus from the dead is living in you, he who raised Christ from the dead will also give life to your mortal bodies through his Spirit, who lives in you" (Rom. 8:11).

The Holy Spirit not only resurrects your old life into a new life but keeps all believers on a steady track until they reach heaven.

77. MY MOM BELIEVES THAT ANGELS ARE EVERYWHERE. I TELL HER THAT ANGELS ARE IN HEAVEN. WHO IS RIGHT?

You both are. Multitudes of angels populate the world. Hebrews 12:22 speaks of "thousands of angels in joyful assembly." Jude declared, "The Lord is coming with thousands and thousands of holy angels to judge everyone" (vv. 14–15 CEV). An inspired King David wrote, "The chariots of God are twenty thousand, even thousands of angels: the Lord is among them, as in Sinai, in the holy place" (Ps. 68:17 KJV). David also spoke of the time ten thousand angels descended on the mountain as God gave the Law to Moses: "GOD came down from Sinai ... coming with ten thousand holy angels" (Deut. 33:2 MSG).

Thousands of angels awaited the call of Christ on the day of the cross. "Do you think that I cannot appeal to My Father, and He will at once put at My disposal more than twelve legions of angels?" (Matt. 26:53 NASB).

Angels minister to God's people. "[God] has put his angels in charge of you to watch over you wherever you go" (Ps. 91:11 NCV). As a believer, you can expect angels to go with you everywhere.

But what if you are not a believer? Do angels offer equal surveillance to God's enemies? No, they don't. The promise of angelic protection is limited to those who trust God. "All the angels are spirits who serve God and are sent to *help those who will receive salvation*" (Heb. 1:14 NCV, emphasis mine). David spoke of this restricted coverage: "For the angel of the LORD is a guard; he surrounds and defends *all who fear him*" (Ps. 34:7 NLT, emphasis mine).

Refuse God at the risk of an unguarded back. But receive his lordship, and be assured that many mighty angels will guard you in all your ways.

78. Does God lead us through feelings? When people say, "I sense God's guidance," what are they describing?

Some years ago Denalyn and I were a signature away from moving from one house to another. The structure was nice, and the price was fair. It seemed a wise move. But I didn't feel peaceful about it. The project stirred unease and restlessness. I finally drove to the builder's office and removed my name from his list. To this day I can't pinpoint the source of the discomfort. I just didn't feel peaceful about it.

A few months ago I was asked to speak at a racial unity conference. I intended to decline but couldn't bring myself to do so. The event kept surfacing in my mind like a cork in a lake. Finally I agreed. Returning from the event, I still couldn't explain the impression to be there. But I felt peaceful about the decision, and that was enough.

Sometimes a choice just "feels" right. When Luke justified the writing of his gospel to Theophilus, he said, "Since I myself have carefully investigated everything from the beginning, it seemed good also to me to write an orderly account for you, most excellent Theophilus" (1:3).

Did you note the phrase "it seemed good also to me"? These words reflect a person standing at the crossroads. Luke pondered his options and selected the path that "seemed good."

Jude did likewise. He intended to dedicate his epistle to the topic of salvation, but he felt uneasy with the choice. Look at the third verse of his letter.

> Dear friends, I wanted very much to write you about the salvation we all share.
> But I felt the need to write you about something else: I want to encourage you
> to fight hard for the faith that was given the holy people of God once and for
> all time. (NCV)

Again the language. "I wanted . . . But I felt . . ." From whence came Jude's feelings? Did they not come from God? The same God who "is working in you to help you want to do . . . what pleases him" (Phil. 2:13 NCV). God creates the "want to" within us.

Be careful with this. People have been known to justify stupidity based on a feeling. "I felt God leading me to cheat on my wife . . . disregard my bills . . . lie to my boss . . . flirt with my married neighbor." Mark it down: God will not lead you to violate his Word. He will not contradict his teaching. Be careful with the phrase "God led me . . ." Don't banter it about. Don't disguise your sin as a leading of God. He will not lead you to lie, cheat, or hurt.

But he will faithfully lead you through the words of his Scripture and the advice of his faithful.

79.
My parents aren't Christians, so it's difficult for me to trust the advice they try to give me about my career choices. How can I find godly wisdom to make good choices?

The fifth commandment does not say, "Honor your God-fearing mother and father who have a Christian worldview." It says, "Honor your father and your mother" (Ex. 20:12). Period. There's no specification about their beliefs. So honor them by at least hearing what they have to say.

Surely you would listen to cooking suggestions from a five-star chef and remodeling tips from an expert handyman even though they weren't Christians. Wisdom is wisdom, and it comes in all shapes and sizes from all kinds of people.

But when the words of the world fall short, *go to the Lord.*

I will guide you along the best pathway for your life.
I will advise you and watch over you. (Ps. 32:8 NLT)

Seek his will in all you do,
    and he will show you which path to take. (Prov. 3:6 NLT)

My sheep listen to my voice; I know them, and they follow me. (John 10:27 NLT)

Then *go to the Bible.*

For the word of God is living and active. Sharper than any double-edged sword, it penetrates even to dividing soul and spirit, joints and marrow; it judges the thoughts and attitudes of the heart. (Heb. 4:12)

God's Word is a living and active counselor in your time of need.

Feeling betrayed? "I will never fail you. I will never abandon you" (Heb. 13:5 NLT).

Feeling anxious? "Do not be anxious about anything, but in everything, by prayer and petition, with thanksgiving, present your requests to God" (Phil. 4:6).

Feeling underappreciated? "Whatever you do, work at it with all your heart, as working for the Lord, not for men" (Col. 3:23).

So listen to your parents; then go to the Lord and his living Word. You can't go wrong with that combination.

80.
OUR CHURCH IS HAVING TROUBLE GETTING ALONG. SIDES ARE BEING DRAWN, AND TEMPERS ARE FLARING. WHAT CAN WE DO?

The church resembles a family on summer vacation. You know the experience. They pile in the car and hit the road. Initially, the enthusiasm soars and moods are good. But three hundred miles of interstate takes a toll. Johnny uses too much of the seat. Heather won't share her pillow. Dad refuses to ask for directions, and Mom has to stop at the restroom again. Candied apples fall on the carpet. Feet smell, and tension swells. There is a time in every trip when each family member has this thought: *I'm getting out of the car. I'll hitchhike. I'll walk. I'll do anything. Just get me out of this car.*

But do we? No, we stay in the car. Why? One, we can't reach the destination alone, and, two, we are family.

Can't the same be said about Christians in a congregation? We don't spill the candy, but we spill the beans. Our feet may not stink, but our attitudes do. We grow weary of one another. Some start to smell. But do we get out of the car?

No. Apart from the Father, we can't reach the destination. And, besides, we are family.

Not always easy, is it? I once saw a person on a religious broadcast with poofy hair and pink clothes and bright shoes, and you should have seen how his wife was dressed. *How can we be in the same family?* I wondered. The answer came as they began to speak. They spoke genuinely of Christ on the cross. They spoke of grace for all sin. I'm not too keen on the way they look, but I love the One to whom they look. And since we look to the same One, are we not family?

Then there is the fellow with whom I disagree about everything. Politics. Ethics. What he sees as important doctrine, I see as tradition. What I see as necessary change, he sees as rocking the boat. I've never known a man with such poor judgment. But each Sunday we sit in the same church. Each Sunday we partake of the same bread and drink of the same cup. And each Sunday I'm reminded: the Lord determines who sits at the table, not me. And if the Lord invites him and me to the same table, are we not family?

We dress differently. We think differently. We are different. But if we're in the same car, being driven by the same Father, headed toward the same place, can we not accept one another?

81.
SOME MEMBERS OF OUR BIBLE STUDY GROUP ARE VERY CRITICAL. THEY BAD-MOUTH ANYONE WHO DISAGREES WITH THEM. THIS BOTHERS ME.

It bothers God too. He says, "Do not argue about opinions" (Rom. 14:1 NCV). It's one thing to have an opinion; it's something else entirely to have a fight. When you sense the volume increasing and the heat rising, close your mouth. It's better to be quiet and keep a brother than be loud and lose one. Besides, "They are God's servants, not yours. They are responsible to him, not to you. Let him tell them whether they are right or wrong. And God is able to make them do as they should" (Rom. 14:4 TLB).

"Stop judging each other" (Rom. 14:13 NCV). We judge others when we stop addressing the controversy and start attacking the character. Example? "Of course she wants women to preach; she's power hungry." Or, "I'm not surprised he likes loud worship; he's one of those rowdy sorts anyway." One more: "You'd expect such an opinion out of a person who never studies the Bible."

These are judgmental phrases. These are off-limits phrases. If we disagree, let's disagree agreeably. Unity demands that we discuss the issue, not the person. And "let us try to do what makes peace and helps one another" (Rom. 14:19 NCV).

"Above all things have fervent love among yourselves; for love shall cover the multitude of sins" (1 Peter 4:8 NEW SCOFIELD BIBLE). If love covers a multitude of sins, can it not cover a multitude of opinions?

82.
My wife and I don't have any friends at church, and we're not involved in any of the activities. We're thinking about just staying at home on Sundays. Would this be wrong?

I know what you mean. I think about staying home some Sundays too . . . *and I'm one of the ministers!*

I wonder what would happen if, as I went to work, my stomach decided to stay home, take a little break. Or if my spleen just needed some time to get its act together. Or if my left foot walked out on me.

I would be a mess. Practically dead. Completely incapacitated.

Ever wonder why Paul refers to the church as the body of Christ?

We are parts of [Christ's] body. (Eph. 5:30 NCV)

[Christ] is the head of the body, which is the church. (Col. 1:18 NCV)

I am not his body; you are not his body. We—together—are his body.

But bodies are so fragile, prone to sickness and rupture. Church bodies are fragile too, prone to envy and insignificance.

If the foot should say, "Because I am not a hand, I am not of the body," is it therefore not of the body? And if the ear should say, "Because I am not an eye, I am not of the body," is it therefore not of the body? If the whole body were an eye, where would be the hearing? If the whole were hearing, where would be the smelling? But now God has set the members, each one of them, in the body just as He pleased. (1 Cor. 12:15–18 NKJV)

Every part of the body is necessary because each serves a function. No part is the whole, but every part is part of the whole. Our world desperately needs people who stick together and love one another. This group is the church.

Is there ever a time to leave a church? Yes. In the event of immoral or dishonest leadership. If the pastors are using or abusing the flock, get out. Otherwise,

brains need to find reasonable answers,

eyes need to see the problems,

stomachs need to digest the situation,

spleens need to get rid of bacteria,
hands need to soothe,
feet need to get to work.
Don't eject yourself from the body . . . or it will die.

83.
SOME PEOPLE IN OUR CHURCH FEEL THAT WE SHOULDN'T ASSOCIATE WITH MEMBERS OF OTHER DENOMINATIONS. THIS DOESN'T SEEM RIGHT TO US, BUT WE ARE NEW BELIEVERS, AND WE WANT TO RESPECT THE OPINIONS OF THOSE WHO HAVE BEEN IN THE CHURCH LONGER THAN WE HAVE.

Some preach a different message than Christianity. Sometimes subtle. Sometimes obvious. Those groups need to be approached with caution since they use twisted theology and convoluted reasoning to confuse the converts.

Within Christianity there are subcategories or denominations that have different ways of expressing biblical truth. One group wears suits, another wears collars, and another wears golf shirts. They may differ in their views of communion: once a week, once a month, or every once in a while. Wine, grape juice, fruit punch. When it comes to baptism, one may immerse, the other sprinkle.

Whatever churches' methods and whatever their practices, God has one flock. The flock has one shepherd. And though we may think there are many, we are wrong. There is only one.

Never in the Bible are we told to create unity. We are told simply to maintain the unity that exists. Paul exhorts us to preserve "the unity which the Spirit gives" (Eph. 4:3 NEB). Our task is not to invent unity but to acknowledge it.

I grew up with two sisters and a brother. We came from the same family. We had the same father and mother. I'm sure there were times when they didn't want to call me their brother, but they didn't have that choice.

Nor do we in the church. When I hear someone calling God "Father" and Jesus "Savior," I meet a brother or a sister—regardless of the name of their church or denomination.

By the way, the church names we banter about? They do not exist in heaven. The Book of Life does not list your denomination next to your name. Why? Because the denomination does not save you. And I wonder, if there are no denominations in heaven, why do we have them on earth?

What would happen . . . (I know this is a crazy thought.) But what would happen if all the churches agreed, on a given day, to change their names simply to "church"? What if any reference to any denomination were removed and we were all just Christians? And then when people chose which church to attend, they wouldn't do so by the sign outside. They'd do so by the hearts of the people inside. And then when people were asked what church they attended, their answer would be just a location, not a label.

And then we Christians wouldn't be known for what divides us; instead, we'd be known for what unites us—our common Father.

84.

SURELY CHRISTIANS, OF ALL PEOPLE, SHOULD BE ABLE TO GET ALONG, BUT THERE ALWAYS SEEM TO BE TWO OR THREE GROUPS IN A CHURCH WHO COMPETE WITH EACH OTHER AND BICKER AND FIGHT. IS THERE ANY HOPE FOR THIS PROBLEM?

Remember the church at Corinth? A problem on every pew! Territorially selfish. Morally shameless. Theologically reckless. And corporately thoughtless. How do you help a congregation like that?

You can correct them. Paul did. You can instruct them, which Paul did. You can reason with them; Paul did. But at some point you stop talking to the head and start appealing to the heart. And Paul did that: "Love . . . bears all things, believes all things, hopes all things, endures all things" (1 Cor. 13:4, 7 NKJV).

He saw only one solution. And that solution was a five-letter Greek word: A-G-A-P-E. *Agape.*

Paul could have used the Greek word *eros.* But he wasn't speaking of sexual love. He could have used the term *phileo,* but he presented far more than friendship. Or he could have used *storge,* a tender term for the love of family. But Paul had more in mind than domestic peace.

He envisioned an *agape* love. *Agape* love cares for others because God has cared for us. *Agape* love goes beyond sentiment and good wishes. Because God loved first, *agape* love responds. Because God was gracious, *agape* love forgives the mistake when the offense is high. *Agape* offers patience when stress is abundant and extends kindness when kindness is rare. Why? Because God offered both to us.

This is the type of love that Paul prescribed for the church in Corinth. Don't we need the same prescription today? Don't groups still fight with each other? Aren't we sometimes quiet when we should speak? And don't those who have found freedom still have the hardest time with those who haven't? Someday there will be a community where everyone behaves and no one complains. But it won't be this side of heaven.

So until then, what do we do? We reason. We confront. We teach. But most of all, we love.

85. HOW ARE WE SUPPOSED TO VIEW CHRISTIANS FROM A DIFFERENT GROUP? SOME OF THEM ACT VERY DIFFERENTLY THAN I DO.

First, look at their fruit. Is it good? Is it healthy? Is he or she helping or hurting people? Production is more important than pedigree. The fruit is more important than the name of the orchard. If the person is bearing fruit, be grateful! A good tree cannot produce bad fruit (Matt. 7:17–18), so be thankful that God is at work in other groups than yours.

But also look at the faith. In whose name is the work done? Jesus accepted the work of the man who cast out demons because it was done in the name of Christ (Mark 9:38–39). What does it mean to do something in the name of Jesus? It means you are under the authority of and empowered by that name.

If I go to a car dealership and say I want a free car, the salespeople are going to laugh at me. If, however, I go with a letter written and signed by the owner of the dealership granting me a free car, then I drive off in a free car. Why? Because I am there under the authority of and am empowered by the owner.

The Master says examine the person's faith. If he or she has faith in Jesus and is empowered by God, grace says that's enough. This is an important point. There are some who do not work in God's name.

But there are believers in many different heritages who cast their hope in God's firstborn Son and put their faith in the cross of Christ. If they, like you, are trusting him to carry them to the Father's castle, don't you share a common Savior? If their trust, like yours, is in the all-sufficient sacrifice of Christ, aren't you covered with the same grace?

You mean they don't have to be in my group? No.

They don't have to share my background? They don't.

They don't have to see everything the way I do? Does anyone?

86.

I LIKE JESUS. I JUST DON'T LIKE HIS FOLLOWERS. AT LEAST I DON'T LIKE THE WAY THEY BEHAVE. ALL THIS "AMEN" AND "PRAISE THE LORD" SEEM PHONY.

You aren't alone. Hypocrisy turns people away from God. When God-hungry souls walk into a congregation of wannabe superstars, what happens? When God-seekers see singers strut like Las Vegas entertainers . . . When they hear the preacher—a man of slick words, dress, and hair—play to the crowd and exclude God . . . When other attendees dress to be seen and make much to-do over their gifts and offerings . . . When people enter a church to see God, yet can't see him because of the church, don't think for a second that God doesn't react. "Be especially careful when you are trying to be good so that you don't make a performance out of it. It might be good theater, but the God who made you won't be applauding" (Matt. 6:1 MSG).

Hypocrisy turns people against God, so he has a no-tolerance policy. Let's take hypocrisy as seriously as God does. How can we?

Expect no credit for good deeds. None. If no one notices, you aren't disappointed. If someone does, you give the credit to God. Ask yourself this question: if no one knew of the good I do, would I still do it? If not, you're doing it to be seen by people.

Give financial gifts in secret. Money stirs the phony within us. We like to be seen earning it. And we like to be seen giving it. So "when you give to someone in need, don't let your left hand know what your right hand is doing" (Matt. 6:3 NLT).

Don't fake spirituality. When you go to church, don't select a seat just to be seen or sing just to be heard. If you raise your hands, raise holy ones, not showy ones. When you talk, don't doctor your vocabulary with trendy religious terms. Nothing nauseates more than a fake "Praise the Lord" or a shallow "Hallelujah" or an insincere "Glory be to God."

Bottom line: don't make a theater production out of your faith.

87.

IN MY ANNUAL JOB PERFORMANCE EVALUATION, MY BOSS TOLD ME TO TRY TO ENCOURAGE PEOPLE MORE. THIS DOESN'T COME NATURALLY OR EASILY. I GUESS I'M A BIT OF A CRITIC. ANY SUGGESTIONS?

Encouragement is no casual, kind word but rather a premeditated resolve to lift the spirits of a friend.

I heard an example of encouragement once in New York City's LaGuardia Airport. The businessman was in the phone carrel next to mine. He didn't know I was listening. I didn't intend to be listening. But I couldn't help it. He was modeling deliberate encouragement.

Apparently he had just closed a big deal and was on his way back to the home office. One by one he was calling the office personnel, sharing the big news and giving each one the credit. He must have spoken to a half dozen workers. With each he began the same way: "Great news. We signed the contract. And I want you to know we couldn't have done it without you. Let me tell you why your role was so important." And then he would proceed to thank them specifically for their work. Receptionist, accountant, vice president—each person was applauded. I don't know who he was, but I know he knew the power of deliberate encouragement.

An encourager does more than slap a few folks on the back. Sometimes he takes a risk on behalf of someone else. That's what Barnabas did. He was such a source of encouragement that the apostles changed his name from Joseph to Barnabas, which means "Son of Encouragement" (Acts 4:36). At no point did he live up to his name more than the day he defended the new convert.

No one else wanted anything to do with the guy. Who would want a murderer in the church? But that's who Saul was. And that's why the apostles were skeptical.

Barnabas, however, practiced deliberate encouragement. "But Barnabas took him and brought him to the apostles. And he declared to them how he [Saul] had seen the Lord on the road, and that He [Jesus] had spoken to him, and how he had preached boldly at Damascus in the name of Jesus. So he was with them at Jerusalem, coming in and going out" (Acts 9:27–28 NKJV).

Suppose Barnabas had stayed quiet. Or suppose Barnabas had followed the crowd. Would the church have ever known Paul?

Every life needs a Barnabas. I *encourage* you to be one to someone else.

88.
WHAT IS THE PURPOSE OF WORSHIP? IT DOESN'T SEEM THAT GOD WOULD NEED US TO SING TO HIM.

The word *worship* conjures up many thoughts in many minds, not all of which are accurate or healthy. When you think of worship, what do you think of?

Outdated songs poorly sung? Dramatic prayers egotistically offered? Irrelevant sermons carelessly delivered? Meager offerings grudgingly given? Near-empty auditoriums and meaningless rituals?

What is worship?

The definition is in the book of Psalms:

> Honor the LORD, you heavenly beings;
> > honor the LORD for his glory and strength.
> Honor the LORD for the glory of his name.
> > Worship the LORD in the splendor of his holiness. (29:1–2 NLT)

The essence of worship is simply this: giving God the honor he deserves. To worship is to applaud the greatness of God.

The ancestry of the English word for *worship* reflects this understanding. This term comes from the Anglo-Saxon word *worthscipe*, which was modified to *worthship* and finally to *worship*. *Worship* means "to attribute worth" to someone or something.

In the context of Scripture, worship is both an attitude and an action. A view of the heart and an event in life.

> Whatever you do, whether in word or deed, do it all in the name of the Lord Jesus, giving thanks to God the Father through him. (Col. 3:17)

This is worship as a lifestyle. Every deed and duty done in such a way that God receives credit and applause. Worship begins as an attitude. But worship deepens as an action.

The action of worship was on the mind of the psalmist when he wrote, "Worship the LORD with gladness; come before him with joyful songs" (Ps. 100:2).

And oh how we need it! We come to worship so bent out of shape. So sold on ourselves that we think someone died and made us king. Or so down on ourselves that we think everyone died and just left us.

We worship because we need it. But this is the secondary reason.

The main reason we worship has nothing to do with us; it has everything to do with God. He deserves to receive it!

89. ONE CHURCH SAYS BAPTISM IS NECESSARY FOR SALVATION. ANOTHER CHURCH SAYS JUST THE OPPOSITE. HOW CAN I KNOW FOR SURE?

Would you feel comfortable marrying someone who wanted to keep the marriage a secret? Neither does God. It's one thing to say in the privacy of your own heart that you are a sinner in need of a Savior, but it's quite another to walk out of the shadows and stand before family, friends, and colleagues and state publicly that Christ is your forgiver and master. This act ups the ante.

Jesus commanded all his followers to prove it, to make the pledge, by public demonstration in baptism. Among his final words was the universal command to "go and make followers of all people in the world. Baptize them in the name of the Father and the Son and the Holy Spirit" (Matt. 28:19 NCV).

Baptism is the initial and immediate step of obedience by the believer. As far as we know, every single convert in the New Testament church was baptized. With the exception of the thief on the cross, there is no example of an unbaptized believer.

The thief on the cross, however, is a crucial exception. His conversion drives dogmatists crazy. It is no accident that the first one to accept the invitation of the crucified Christ had no creed, confirmation, christening, or catechism. How disturbing to theologians to ascend the mountain of doctrine only to be greeted by a thief who cast his lot with Christ. Here is a man who never went to church, never gave an offering, never was baptized, and only said one prayer, but that prayer was enough (Luke 23:33–43).

The thief reminds us that, in the end, it is Jesus who saves. Does the thief's story negate the importance of baptism? No, it simply puts baptism in proper perspective. Any step taken is a response to a salvation offered, not an effort to earn salvation. In the end Jesus has the right to save any heart, for he, and only he, sees the heart.

90.

MY FRIEND HAS REALLY GONE OFF THE DEEP END. SHE USED TO WALK WITH GOD. NOW SHE HANGS WITH A BAD CROWD AND DOES THINGS I CAN'T BELIEVE SHE DOES. BUT I DON'T KNOW HOW TO HELP HER.

On the walkie-talkie of a firefighter is an RIT button. RIT stands for "Rapid Intervention Team." A firefighter presses this button only when he is hemmed in by danger and has no hope of escape. The moment he sends an RIT signal, his fellow firefighters stop what they are doing and come to his rescue. The fire becomes secondary. All resources are focused on one objective: get the man out of danger.

God has a Rapid Intervention Team as well. And you may be on it. Look at the rescue personnel. "You who are spiritual should restore him" (Gal. 6:1).

Typically we assume that rescue is the role of the leaders. Most often it is. Most often the elders, teachers, and ministers are called into duty when someone goes down. But the apostle Paul does not limit Rapid Intervention Teams to leaders. You may be a quiet but godly church member who has noticed the absence of someone.

Whoever you are, if you are *spiritual* (walking with God), God will deputize you. When he calls you, the purpose of your mission is restoration. "You who are spiritual should *restore* him."

The goal is restoration, not castigation or humiliation. The rescuer approaches the intervention carefully, "lest [he] also be tempted" (v. 1 NKJV), and he should graciously "restore such a one in a spirit of gentleness" (v. 1 NKJV).

Let's see if we can envision the rescue. Let's say a woman in the church gets tangled up in a mess. Things between her and her husband were chilly, so when things between her and her coworker got warm, she fell. She fell into the arms of another man.

That was bad. What was worse is that she didn't feel bad. Chalk it up to midlife, stress at work, struggle at home, or whatever, but she didn't feel bad, and she didn't change. By the time anyone at church found out, she was out. A husband and a couple of kids were left bobbing in her wake.

Can you imagine a worse scenario? I can. What if she didn't belong to a church? What if she wasn't known or active? What if her friends at church didn't take their roles seriously?

But she did, she was, and they did. They knocked on her door. They sent her notes. They made calls. They wouldn't give up. Finally she agreed to see a counselor. The healing wasn't immediate, but it was eventual. And, in time, she went home. A sister was restored, a family saved. The reputation of Christ was upheld, and the law of Jesus was fulfilled. "Bear one another's burdens, and so fulfill the law of Christ" (v. 2 NKJV).

God's plan is simple. When a believer falls, the church responds. Immediately. Honestly. Gently.

Him/Her

Sex, Romance, and "Any chance
of a second chance?"

Lisa —

I'll be praying for you
and your husband. Please,
search your hearts for
forgiveness. You'll never give
more grace than God has
already given. Ask God
to heal your marriage. He
raised His son from the
dead — who's to say He won't
do the same with your
marriage —

Max

91. IT'S MY BODY, ISN'T IT? AS LONG AS MY SEXUAL ACTIVITY IS CONSENSUAL, WHAT'S THE HARM?

Casual sex—intimacy outside of marriage—pretends we can give the body and not affect the soul. We can't. We humans are so intricately psychosomatic that whatever touches the *soma* (body) impacts the psyche as well. The me-centered phrase "as long as no one gets hurt" sounds noble, but the truth is, we don't know who gets hurt.

Consider God's plan. A man and a woman make a public covenant with each other. They disable the ejection seats. They burn the bridge back to Mama's house. They fall into each other's arms beneath the canopy of God's blessing, encircled by the tall fence of fidelity. Both know the other will be there in the morning. Both know the other will stay even as skin wrinkles and vigor fades. Each gives the other exclusive for-your-eyes-only privileges. Gone is the guilt. Gone the undisciplined lust.

What remains is a celebration of permanence, a tender moment in which the body continues what the mind and the soul have already begun. A time in which "the man and his wife were both naked and were not ashamed" (Gen. 2:25 NASB). Such sex honors God.

God-centered thinking rescues us from the sex we thought would make us happy. You may think your dalliances are harmless, and years may pass before the X-rays reveal the internal damage, but don't be fooled. Casual sex is a diet of chocolate—it tastes good for a while, but the imbalance can ruin you. Sex apart from God's plan wounds the soul.

Sex according to God's plan nourishes it.

92. IN MY OPINION, PREMARITAL SEX PREPARES THE COUPLE FOR MARRIAGE. WOULDN'T YOU WANT THE SOON-TO-BE-MARRIED COUPLE TO KNOW EACH OTHER AS WELL AS POSSIBLE?

What does premarital sex tell you about a person? Do you learn anything about his character? About her patience? Does a night of passion answer these questions: "Will he love my kids?" "Will she tell the truth?" "Will we love God better together than apart?"

Hardly. Premarital sex reveals only one thing: this person likes to sleep around. And it tells your partner the same thing about you.

Courtship sex doesn't enhance a relationship; it stunts its growth. It shifts the attention from the study of the soul to fascination with the body. Necessary friendship creation is neglected. Essential communication tools go underdeveloped. Most of all, spiritual intimacy takes a backseat to physical intimacy. The purpose of courting is to know each other's souls, not bodies.

God calls for presexual marriage. "So a man will leave his father and mother and be united with his wife, and the two will become one body" (Gen. 2:24 NCV). The leaving is the announcement that a man and woman make to the community. Whether this announcement occurs in a cathedral ceremony or a backyard wedding, it serves the same purpose. It declares a covenant between two people. It removes two individuals from the dating market and enrolls them in the university of matrimony.

Leaving, uniting, then sex. First comes love, then comes marriage, then comes the fruit of love . . . the baby carriage.

93.
MY SPOUSE AND I HAVE UNEVEN SEXUAL INTERESTS. MY "NOW?"
IS OFTEN RETURNED WITH A "NO." ANY ADVICE?

There are times when one spouse just "isn't there." There are occasions when the interest levels don't meet. One is more enthused than the other. Don't make your spouse feel guilty or manipulated. Let the servant spirit reign.

Communicate. If something is burdening you, open up. Let your mate know what troubles you. Maybe you could suggest a different plan. Explain to your spouse that you are tired tonight but are known to get frisky with the sunrise. Or lower your expectations for the evening. Marital sex is like evening meals: sometimes we snack; sometimes we feast. Healthy marriages learn to serve hors d'oeuvres when a Thanksgiving dinner isn't possible. Wives, you can be responsive even if you are not totally engaged. Husbands, you can be patient even if you had your hopes high.

But what if the disinterest lasts longer than a few days? The arrival of kids disrupts not just sleep patterns but available energy. Some men avoid intimacy for fear of failure. Commercials tell them they need to "perform" and ask them, "Will you be ready?" For fear they won't be, they avoid the possibility. Some wives avoid sex because it drudges up memories of abuse or mistakes. Physiological issues like stress and depression can diminish interest in intimacy for weeks at a time. The causes of extended sexual inactivity are manifold. A cure might route you through a counselor's or doctor's office, but the cure always begins with mutual understanding. "It takes wisdom to have a good family, and it takes understanding to make it strong" (Prov. 24:3 NCV).

"Marriage is not a place to 'stand up for your rights.' Marriage is a decision to serve the other, whether in bed or out" (1 Cor. 7:4 MSG).

Absence of sex can be endured. Absence of discussing the absence cannot. Somebody needs to speak up. Both need to look up . . . look up to God for help. You are not without solutions.

94.
NO ONE WARNED MY WIFE AND ME ABOUT THE WHOLE SEXUAL DIFFERENCES THING. I THINK THIS DISCUSSION SHOULD BE IN ALL PREMARITAL CLASSES. WE ARE SORTING IT OUT, BUT IT WAS A SURPRISING CHALLENGE.

Men and women are different. We love that.

Men and women are different. We hate that!

Love or hate the differences, let's understand them.

Wives, understand that your husband sees sex as a primary need. Men, understand that your wife sees sex as optional. In one study when men were asked to rank the importance of sex, they consistently scored it 1, 2, or 3. (I think some scored it 1, 2, *and* 3.) Women, on average, ranked sex in the number 13 slot—right behind "gardening together."[1] Apparently the presence of a good garden indicates a restless husband.

Men and women are different. Men categorize the sexual experience. The husband can have a horrible day, be anticipating World War III the next, hear a tornado outside, and still enjoy sex right now.

The wife doesn't as quickly detach or disentangle from the demands of life. And she may take offense that her husband does. "How can you think about that at a time like this?"

His response: "It's easy."

She thinks he is insensitive. He thinks she's a prude. Neither is right. Both can understand the other better. Take a servant attitude into your sex life. "Give each other more honor than you want for yourselves" (Rom. 12:10 ncv).

Here's another example. Men, about once a month, your wife's body passes through an inward mutiny. Her moods can swing, and her body becomes sensitive. Her irritability is some form of internal rebooting. Be patient during these days. She endures your outbursts over lost football games or rained-out fishing trips. You can be supportive too.

Wives, when it comes to sexual stimuli, your husbands live in a Las Vegas light show. Telling him not to think so much about sex is like telling him to ignore doughnuts in a Krispy Kreme shop. It's everywhere—magazines, billboards, television, movies. Why, companies use curvy models to sell bass boats. Be patient and pray for him.

In fact, pray about this issue. Kneel at the bed together and pray: "Lord, this is your will and your marriage. Help us honor you in this bed."

I know; it's a prayer rarely prayed. Which could be the reason for so many conflicts.

95. WHAT SEXUAL ITEMS AND ACTIVITIES ARE ACCEPTABLE TO GOD? NEGLIGEES? BODY OILS? ENGAGING IN SPECIFIC ACTIVITIES, USING SENSUAL LANGUAGE, AND WATCHING STIMULATING MOVIES? WHAT DOES GOD PROHIBIT AND PERMIT?

First of all, dismiss the notion that God is anti-sex, anti-affection, or anti-intercourse. After all, he developed the package. Sex is a part of his plan. Sex is practical: it populates the earth. Sex is personal: it strengthens a marriage. Sex is pictorial: it symbolizes the bond between husband and wife and between Christ and the church. Sex is powerful. Properly used, it can heal the heart. Improperly administered, it can ravage a life.

We know what God prohibits:

~ Any sexual activity outside of marriage (1 Cor. 7:2; 1 Thess. 4:3)
~ Unbridled lustful passion for someone who is not your spouse (Matt. 5:28)
~ Obscenity and crude language (Eph. 4:29)

Pass your questions through these filters. Someone asks, for example, about using sensual language in moments of intimacy. "Let nothing foul or dirty come out of your mouth. Say only what helps, each word a gift" (Eph. 4:29 MSG). Are you using words that build up your mate and honor God? If so, use them. Do your words degrade your mate? Do they reflect the language of evil more than the vernacular of God? If so, you know what to do.

Some wonder about certain practices and activities in marital sex. With the exception of the Song of Songs, Scripture says very little. God gives his children license to enjoy each other in any fashion that mutually upbuilds. But if one spouse feels degraded or uncomfortable, it is not the place of the other to insist on his own way. "Just because something is technically legal doesn't mean that it's spiritually appropriate" (1 Cor. 6:12 MSG). What is permissible is not always beneficial.

See sex as a chance to serve your mate, not use your mate.

Sexual drives are strong, but marriage is strong enough to contain them and provide for a balanced and fulfilling sexual life in a world of sexual disorder. The marriage bed must be a place of mutuality—the husband seeking to satisfy his wife, the wife seeking to satisfy her husband. Marriage is not a place to "stand up for your rights." Marriage is a decision to serve the other, whether in bed or out. (1 Cor. 7:2–4 MSG)

96.

OUR MARRIAGE IS MARRED BY BETRAYAL. WE DON'T TRUST EACH OTHER ANYMORE. ADULTERY HAS LEFT US DISTANT AND BITTER. WE DON'T AGREE ON MUCH, BUT WE AGREE ON THIS: OUR MARRIAGE IS A MESS.

Let me direct my answer to the different parties.

Have you failed your spouse? If so, own up to it. Don't minimize or deny it. Confess it and seek the forgiveness of each person you have hurt. Then give them time to mend. It's not up to you to determine the recovery period. Don't attempt to dictate the time it takes for a heart to heal.

Suppose you are a company bookkeeper who has embezzled two thousand dollars a month for two years. Then, under conviction, you confess your crime to your boss. You are genuinely sorry. And the first day after your admission you show up at work to continue your job. You expect your supervisor to entrust you with the company finances. How will the boss react? He may give you a broom, but he's not going to trust you with the books.

When you violated your marital covenant, you lost the trust of your spouse. Your confession may make you feel better. But your confession broke the heart of the one you hurt. The burden you got off your chest landed on the shoulders of your spouse. And your spouse needs time to recover. How much time? As long as it takes.

Has your spouse failed you? As difficult as it may seem and as impossible as it may appear, forgiveness is your goal. Seek to give your spouse what God has given to you—grace. Your marriage can be saved and intimacy restored, in time, as you are "kind and compassionate to one another, forgiving each other, just as in Christ God forgave you" (Eph. 4:32).

What your spouse did was despicable, but who your spouse is, is essential. Your mate is God's child, bought by Christ and known by heaven. See less of your spouse's mistake and more of God's grace, and, with time, healing will come.

Have you failed you? Does shame from your youth hound you? Or mistakes from last week dog you? Unaddressed guilt stirs misdirected anger and unhealthy shame. It prompts people to lash out at and withdraw from those they love. Take your moral failures to God's throne of grace.

He restores spiritual virginity. He lifts his children to a blameless place. Remember the words of Paul? "Because of the sacrifice of the Messiah, his blood poured out on the altar of the Cross, we're a free people—free of penalties and punishments chalked up by all our misdeeds. And not just barely free, either. *Abundantly* free!" (Eph. 1:7 MSG).

Let God cleanse you. Tell God the name of the persons or the occasion of the pornography. Bring the moments into the light of God's grace. Sexual sin requires specific confession because it affects us so deeply. "There is a sense in which sexual sins are different from all others. In sexual sin we violate the sacredness of our own bodies, these bodies that were made for God-given and God-modeled love, for 'becoming one' with another" (1 Cor. 6:18 MSG).

His grace is sufficient, and his mercy is ample. His word to you is his word to the ancients:

> Forget about what's happened;
>   don't keep going over old history.
> Be alert, be present. I'm about to do something brand-new.
>   It's bursting out! Don't you see it?
> There it is! I'm making a road through the desert,
>   rivers in the badlands. (Isa. 43:18–19 MSG)

97.

Is it natural for men to ogle women? My husband enjoys looking at attractive women, and he does it even when I'm around. This makes me angry, and I feel humiliated. Don't I have the right to ask him to stop doing this?

Jesus had this to say, and he was a man!

> You have heard that it was said, "Do not commit adultery." But I tell you that anyone who looks at a woman lustfully has already committed adultery with her in his heart. If your right eye causes you to sin, gouge it out and throw it away. It is better for you to lose one part of your body than for your whole body to be thrown into hell. (Matt. 5:27–29)

Lust means looking at a person with sexual intent, fantasizing about someone you are not married to.

Adultery means that, as a married person, you are engaging in sexual activity with someone other than your spouse.

What's the difference? Touch.

What's the similarity? Thought.

I've heard it said that lust is the second time you gaze at a woman. There's some wisdom in that.

Jesus made the same point about lust that he made about murder (Matt. 5:21). The only difference between the mental contemplation of hate and the act of murder is that murder pulls the trigger. The thought process is the same.

Both lust and hate cross a line. Sin is as much thought as it is action. Unbridled anger can lead to first-degree murder. Unmanaged thoughts about sex can lead to physical adultery.

Lust also threatens the spouse. For just a second, that bathing-suit beauty becomes the most attractive woman in the world, not you. For a fleeting moment, that brawny muscle man becomes the biggest stud who ever lived, not you.

That hurts. It is humiliating.

Let your spouse know how it feels. "Every time you talk about another woman, it hurts me." "Every time you talk that way, I feel ugly."

Hopefully, next time he will think twice about looking twice.

98.

WHAT IS THE BIG DEAL ABOUT PORNOGRAPHY? WHY MAKE SUCH A BIG DEAL OUT OF WHAT IS NATURAL? SOME MEN SAY THEY ARE CONTROLLED BY PORNOGRAPHY. NOT ME. I CAN SAMPLE WITHOUT STRUGGLING. SO I DO.

Pornography is thievery. You are stealing glances at women who don't belong to you. When you flip through the lingerie magazine or porn channel, you are committing grand larceny.

Don't be fooled! You are not as strong as you think. You can't stop where you want to stop. You can't play with fire and not get burned. So don't light the match. "For lust is a shameful sin, a crime that should be punished. It is a fire that burns all the way to hell" (Job 31:11–12 NLT).

Job accompanies his warning with an example: "I made a solemn pact with myself never to undress a girl with my eyes" (Job 31:1 MSG).

The Bible never says to battle sexual sin, struggle against sexual sin . . . no, our call is to "run away from sexual sin" (1 Cor. 6:18 NCV).

Just because a woman dresses to lure, you don't have to look. Just because pictures appear, you don't have to view them. You can't keep a bird from flying over your roof, but you can screen them out of your chimney. Put the two-second rule into effect. The next time you see more than you should in a picture, on a screen, or in the window of a Victoria's Secret store, give yourself two seconds to reengage. You have two ticks of the clock to come to your senses and shift your gaze. Guard your thoughts! "God has not called us to be dirty-minded and full of lust, but to be holy and clean" (1 Thess. 4:7 TLB).

You will live tomorrow the thoughts you tolerate today. Use this to your advantage! Want a stronger marriage tomorrow? Ponder the strengths of your mate today. Want to enjoy more faith tomorrow? Meditate on God's Word today. Desire a guilt-free future? Then saturate the present in grace. You are what you think. "People harvest only what they plant" (Gal. 6:7 NCV). So select your seeds carefully.

99.

I WAS SAVED OUT OF A VERY SINFUL LIFESTYLE, WHICH MEANT I WAS FAR FROM INNOCENT WHEN I GOT MARRIED TWO YEARS AGO. MY HUSBAND WAS A VIRGIN WHEN WE MARRIED. HE KNEW ABOUT MY PAST, AND I THOUGHT HE HAD FORGOTTEN ALL ABOUT IT. BUT NOW IT SEEMS AS THOUGH HE'S HAVING A HARD TIME WITH IT. HE KEEPS BRINGING IT UP, AND THIS IS WREAKING HAVOC WITH OUR SEX LIFE.

There's an old saying: "Love never forgets."

Or is it "Love always forgets"?

I can't remember.

Love never forgets the other person, remembering the reasons that brought them together, keeping them in mind all the time. Love never forgets the sacrifices and the expressions of heartfelt devotion.

Love should forget the mistakes, the wrongdoings, the sin. But it can't. We can't force ourselves to have amnesia. Neither can God.

God cannot forget our sins, but he chooses not to dwell on them. He prefers to see his Son living in us, since Jesus' sacrifice covers our sins (Gal. 2:20). He sees us as we are now—sanctified, redeemed, and righteous—instead of who we were before. God puts away the photo albums and prefers to see us live and in person.

We need to forgive the same way and choose not to dwell on one another's failures. Over time, as we refuse to bring those sins to mind, they get lost in the lists of positive qualities we ponder day in and day out.

You may not have been perfect when you married, but you were perfected by the work of Jesus Christ on the cross. While your husband remained a virgin in his body, he probably did not remain a virgin in his mind and thus needed the same perfecting work of Jesus in his life.

Just as you would not hold his lustful thoughts against him, he should not hold your lustful lifestyle against you. In God's eyes, they are the same. Sin is sin, and both need to be forgiven and put away in the memory drawer.

100.
SOME PEOPLE SAY THAT BEING GAY IS A SIN, AND OTHERS SAY THAT IT'S OKAY IF THE PERSON LOVES GOD. SO DOES GOD HATE HOMOSEXUALS? ALSO, ARE THE COMMANDMENTS IN THE BIBLE ARCHAIC, SPEAKING MORE OF THE CULTURE OF THAT TIME AND NOT NECESSARILY OURS TODAY?

Healthy discussions about homosexuality seem increasingly rare. On one hand we hear harsh, cruel attacks against members of the gay community. Homosexuals are singled out as the butt of jokes or characterized as God-haters. Some homosexuals hate Christians because they think Christians hate them. I honestly cannot imagine what it must be like to hear Christians shout: "Stop your sinning! You are a sinner!" To be called "fag" or "queer" by people who claim to follow Jesus. Travesty. This treatment is tragic and wrong.

Equally concerning is the tendency to discard Scripture's teaching on the topic as irrelevant and outdated. For those of us who hold an authoritative view of the Bible, this is unsettling.

So where does that leave us? Perhaps with these questions:

Were Jesus to come face-to-face with a homosexual, what would he say? What would he do? Though the New Testament contains no such conversation, we do know how he would act.

He would express his love. As he did with Zacchaeus, he might go to his home. As with the Samaritan woman, he might sit with her in the shade of a well. As he did with Matthew, Jesus might offer a personal invitation. The exact words he would use, we don't know. But of their sentiment, we have no doubt. *Jesus loves his gay children.* Nothing can separate us from the love of God. This includes homosexuality. He made them, came for them, and died for them. And he would tell them so.

He would speak to them with compassion. But he would also speak to them with conviction. As he did with Zacchaeus, the Samaritan woman, Matthew, and others, Jesus always told the truth. And the truth is this: God never approves sexual union outside of a heterosexual marriage. The two unmarried but sexually involved singles? God disapproves. The two married people who are sexually involved but not married to each other? Their adultery angers God. The sibling with sibling? The man with multiple wives. The man with man or woman with woman? The Bible never singles out same-sex intimacy as a sin above other sins.

At the same time the Bible never minces words regarding God's feelings toward homosexual activity. God warned the men of Israel: "You shall not lie with a male as with a woman. It is an abomination" (Lev. 18:22 NKJV). One professor wrote: "When the word *toevah* [abomination] does appear in the Hebrew Bible, it is sometimes applied to idolatry, cult prostitution, magic, or divination . . . It always conveys great repugnance."[2] Has God gotten over his repugnance? In the New Testament he called such behavior "shameful" (Rom.1:26 NLT).

This is, for many, a challenging teaching. The temptations are strong, and lures are many. But we must remember that our bodies belong to God. "Your body is a temple for the Holy Spirit who is in you. You have received the Holy Spirit from God. So you do not belong to yourselves, because you were bought by God for a price. So honor God with your bodies" (1 Cor. 6:19–20 NCV). Again, this instruction is not limited to those who struggle with homosexuality. This teaching is for us all.

But isn't such teaching archaic? Some Bible students want to clump the prohibition of homosexuality with cultural instructions like washing feet or wearing veils. If teachings against same-sex unions were random or sporadic, we'd have to agree. But from the earliest code of the Torah to the later epistles of Paul, the sentiment never changes. From start to finish, Scripture categorically condemns same-sex intimacy. From start to finish, Scripture emphasizes God's love for sinners, no matter who they are.

Let's follow the example of Jesus: let's love each other. Talk. Dialog. Jesus went to the home of Zaccheus, spent the afternoon with the Samaritan woman, attended Matthew's party. He didn't endorse their behavior, but he built a bridge to their hearts. Maybe we will find a way to do the same.

101.

I'M SINGLE AND LOVING IT. SOMEDAY, HOWEVER, I WANT TO SETTLE DOWN AND HAVE A FAMILY. I'VE SEEN ENOUGH BAD MARRIAGES TO MAKE ME WONDER WHAT I CAN DO TO HAVE A GOOD ONE. HOW CAN I SELECT THE RIGHT MATE?

A person makes two big decisions in life. The first has to do with faith. The second has to do with family. The first question is, "Who is my God?" The second, "Who, if anyone, will be my spouse?" The first question defines the second. Your God defines your family. If your God is yourself, then you call your own shots because your marriage is for your pleasure and nothing more. But if your God is Christ, then he calls the shots because your marriage is for his honor.

Does that surprise you? You thought marriage was all about you? It's not. Marriage is God's idea. He created it because most of us are better God-followers with a partner than we are alone. Most of us are more effective with our gifts, more faithful in our convictions, more fruitful in our service if we are not living alone. Since marriage is God's idea, wouldn't you think he has an idea as to whom we should marry? He does.

> Don't team up with those who are unbelievers. How can righteousness be a partner with wickedness? How can light live with darkness? (2 Cor. 6:14 NLT)

When my wife, Denalyn, and I climb into the same car, we must agree on the destination. We may disagree on the food we eat. We may disagree on the number of stops we make. We may even disagree on what music to play. But if she wants to go to Mexico and I want to go to Colorado, we have a problem.

Marry someone who loves God more than you do. If you and your spouse don't agree on the goal of the journey, you will have problems. If his goal is to be rich and your goal is to go to heaven . . . if her aim in life is retirement and your aim in life is serving God . . . you will have issues.

- ~ "But I'm so attracted to him. I can convert him." You aren't called to missionary dating.
- ~ "We're not serious, just having a good time." When your definitions of a good time aren't the same, who wins?
- ~ "But I want to get married so badly . . ." You think no marriage is bad? Try a bad marriage.

~ "Have you seen the options among Christians?" God has plans you've never seen.

> Take delight in the LORD,
>> and he will give you your heart's desires. (Ps. 37:4 NLT)

The longer you date a nonbeliever, the longer you postpone the opportunity for God to bring the right person your way. If you are a child of God and you marry a child of the Devil, you're going to have trouble with your father-in-law.

102.

I'VE BEEN DATING A GIRL FOR THREE MONTHS. SHE SAYS SHE IS IN LOVE. I'M NOT SURE I AM, BUT I FEEL DIFFERENT WHEN I'M WITH HER. IS THAT LOVE?

Feelings can fool you. I spoke recently with a teenage girl who was puzzled by the lack of feelings she had for a guy. Before they started dating, she was wild about him. The minute he showed interest in her, however, she lost interest.

I'm thinking also of a young mom. Being a parent isn't as romantic as she anticipated. Diapers and midnight feedings aren't any fun, and she's feeling guilty because they aren't. *Am I low on love?* she wonders.

How do you answer such questions? Ever wish you had a way to assess the quality of your affection? A DNA test for love? Paul offers us one: "Love does not delight in evil but rejoices with the truth" (1 Cor. 13:6). In this verse lies a test for love.

Want to separate the fake from the factual, the counterfeit from the real thing? Want to know if what you feel is genuine love? Ask yourself this: *Do I encourage this person to do what is right?* For true love "takes no pleasure in other people's sins but delights in the truth" (1 Cor. 13:6 JERUSALEM BIBLE).

For instance, one lady calls another and says, "We're friends, right?"

"Yeah, we're friends."

"If my husband asks, you tell him we were together at the movies last night."

"But we weren't."

"I know, but I was, well, I was with another guy, and—hey, you'll do this for me, won't you? We're friends, right? Tighter than sisters, right?"

Does this person pass the test? No way. Love doesn't ask someone to do what is wrong. How do we know? "Love does not delight in evil but rejoices with the truth."

If you find yourself prompting evil in others, heed the alarm. This is not love. And if others prompt evil in you, be alert.

Here's an example. A classic one. A young couple is on a date. His affection goes beyond her comfort zone. She resists. But he tries to persuade her with the oldest line in the book: "But I love you. I just want to be near you. If you loved me . . ."

That siren you hear? It's the phony-love detector. This guy doesn't love her. He may love having sex with her. He may love her body. He may love boasting to his buddies about his conquest. But he doesn't love her. True love will never ask the "beloved" to do what he or she thinks is wrong.

Love doesn't tear down the convictions of others. Quite the contrary.

Love builds up. (1 Cor. 8:1)

Whoever loves a brother or sister lives in the light and will not cause anyone to stumble. (1 John 2:10 NCV)

When you sin against other believers by encouraging them to do something they believe is wrong, you are sinning against Christ. (1 Cor. 8:12 NLT)

Do you want to know if your love for someone is true? If your friendship is genuine? Ask yourself: do I influence this person to do what is right?
If you answered yes, ask her out for dinner.

103.
OUR DAUGHTER IS MAKING FINAL PREPARATIONS FOR HER WEDDING DAY. SHE'S A GODLY WOMAN AND IS MARRYING A WONDERFUL CHRISTIAN MAN, BUT WITH SO MANY MARRIAGES ENDING IN DIVORCE THESE DAYS, WE WORRY EVEN FOR THIS YOUNG COUPLE. CAN YOU GIVE US ONE IMPORTANT PIECE OF ADVICE TO SHARE WITH HER ON HER WEDDING DAY?

Tell her to be patient.

Everything worthwhile takes time to make. Wine. Sculptures. Paintings. Bridges.

However, we want our spouse and our marriage to be perfect the first morning of the honeymoon. We want the perfect house painted the perfect color on the perfect street in Perfect Town, USA. We want to work the perfect job that pays the perfect salary and allows us to work with perfect people. We want the perfect kids to get perfect grades and pick the perfect college.

Sound perfect? Sure.

Sound probable? No.

Be patient. Your spouse, your job, your home, your kids will not be perfect, at least not right away. Over time and with hard work, things fall into place. Maybe not perfect, but perfectly all right.

God is not finished with you yet. He's still working out the kinks in your marriage. He's putting the final touches on your kids. Your home is a work in progress.

Be patient and don't give up before the Master nods approvingly, "Well done."

104.
I DREAD GOING HOME AT THE END OF THE DAY. OUR HOME IS A COMBAT ZONE. I DON'T KNOW WHAT TO DO ABOUT IT. I OFFER TO GO TO COUNSELING, BUT SHE REFUSES. HELP!

No one wants to live in a combat zone. But many do. Many do because they married someone who is so different from them. The quiet marry the boisterous. The laid-back marry the high-strung. The left-brained marry the right-brained. We are attracted to our opposite. But what attracts us when we are dating, attacks us when we are married.

For that reason a good marriage is hard work. Harmony doesn't just happen. Vocal harmony is achieved when the choir practices. Color harmony is achieved when the artist experiments. And marital harmony exists when two people resolve to "make every effort to keep the unity of the Spirit" (Eph. 4:3). Here are some ideas.

Be considerate. "Husbands, in the same way be considerate as you live with your wives" (1 Peter 3:7). The word *consider* shares ancestry with the word *knowledge.* It means to "have an understanding of." It is amazing how quickly consideration vanishes once we get married. "The wisdom that comes from heaven is . . . considerate" (James 3:17). When I'm inconsiderate to my wife, I'm stupid. The wise thing is to be considerate of your husband, of your wife.

Love "does not demand its own way" (1 Cor. 13:5 NLT). Don't try to change your mate. Don't change the "I do" into an "I'll redo." Meet in the middle. Be flexible. Yield your rights. Give and take. Learn the art of negotiation. Compromise.

Keep courting. What you did to fall in love, keep doing so you'll stay in love. "May you rejoice in the wife of your youth" (Prov. 5:18). "Enjoy life with your wife, whom you love" (Eccl. 9:9). Enjoy your spouse. Encourage each other. Compliment your wife on her new shoes, your husband on his hard work. Look into your spouse's eyes and say, "My life is so much better with you." Each day this week pick out something you like, big or small, and be thankful. You will find that your spouse is 90 percent awesome and 10 percent under construction. You have a great spouse. Tell him or her. If there was more courting in marriage, there would be fewer marriages in court.

Fight fairly. Never criticize your spouse in public. When you make fun of her cooking or his snoring, you are hitting below the belt. Let others mock their mates, not you. You signed on for better or for worse; if you can love the worst, things will get better. Don't hide stones in snowballs. Don't harbor grudges or dredge up the past. Avoid unnecessary absolutes like *never* and *always*. When a fight starts, be quick to listen and slow to speak. Honor each other.

Lock the escape hatch. Throw away the key. You must assume "I'm in it till death do us part. I made a promise to God, and I'm going to keep it if it kills me!" Commitment is what makes a marriage great. If divorce is an option, then you're not going to put forth the effort. Don't use the threat of divorce when you get ticked off. When you get mad, you don't hint at leaving. And you don't use scare words. They are off-limits, unacceptable. No matter how mad you are and how angry and how much you hate that person at the moment, you do not bring up the issue of divorce, because it's not even an issue.

Ask Christ to put his Spirit within you. Love Christ even more than you love each other. When the husband focuses on growing toward Christ and the wife focuses on growing toward Christ, it automatically brings them together. Christ is not going to fight with Christ.

105.
My husband says I am too critical of him, and he's right. I have a terrible habit of criticizing him for everything. I hate having this judgmental attitude, and I know it's not good for our marriage. I need help to change my perspective.

Five times in Proverbs, Solomon addresses a quarrelsome wife and twice likens her to a constant dripping and the other times says it's better for a man to live on the roof or in the desert than in the house with her (Prov. 19:13; 21:9, 19; 25:24; 27:15).

Every time a wife nags, drip.

Every time she criticizes, drip.

Every time she blames, drip.

A critical nature can wear on a guy.

You are saying you don't trust your husband to change the situation. He feels it. A man wants to be respected. When he's respected, he leads. When he's challenged, he fights.

You are also saying you don't trust God to change your husband. You forget about praying to God and go straight to criticizing your husband. It's faster, and it gets the point across more quickly. Is that the best path? No.

A man needs to ripen from the inside before he is fruitful. Let God be the critical one. Allow the Holy Spirit to remind your husband of what he needs to do and how he needs to do it.

Do it before your house is flooded and everyone drowns!

106.

IS THERE A BIBLICAL WAY TO HANDLE FINANCES IN A MARRIAGE? MY WIFE DOES A FAR BETTER JOB OF HANDLING OUR FINANCES THAN I EVER COULD. I'M HAPPY (RELIEVED, IN FACT) THAT SHE IS WILLING TO DO THIS. BUT MY BROTHER FEELS STRONGLY THAT THIS IS A GODLY MAN'S RESPONSIBILITY. IS HE RIGHT?

The New Testament gives two commands to husbands about their wives.

Love them (Eph. 5:25, 28; Col. 3:19).

Lead them (Eph. 5:22, 24; Col. 3:18; Titus 2:5; 1 Peter 3:1).

Love them and lead them; that's it.

Nothing about balancing the checkbook.

What's wrong with a husband who likes to clean the house or a wife who enjoys mowing the lawn? If a wife cleans out the garage, has the man been emasculated? Surely not.

If a husband loves his wife and cooks her dinner, is he less of a man than if he changes the oil? So a man loves cooking oil over motor oil! What's the big deal?

If your wife enjoys balancing the checkbook and taking care of the finances, let her. If you love her, encourage her to do something she loves.

Together, work out guidelines for spending. Pray with each other over big purchases. Determine the best investments you can both make.

A real man leads his wife to the things she loves to do.

107.

ALMOST EVERY YEAR WE MOVE TO A NEW HOUSE IF NOT A NEW COUNTRY. MY HUSBAND IS IN THE MILITARY, AND I SUPPORT HIS CAREER COMPLETELY, BUT ALL THE CHANGES THAT COME WITH THESE MOVES ARE BEGINNING TO WEIGH ON ME. I'M BECOMING ANXIOUS ABOUT THE NEXT MOVE, MAKING IT DIFFICULT FOR ME TO BE SUPPORTIVE OF MY HUSBAND.

Life comes caffeinated with surprises. Modifications. Transitions. Alterations. You move down the ladder, out of the house, over for the new guy, up through the system. All this moving. Some changes are welcome; others are not.

While the idea of moving to a new place sounds exotic at first, I'm sure over time it's a burden. As soon as you find your favorite grocery store, you're changing your driver's license. As soon as you memorize the channels on your cable system, you're packing the TV. The minute you've worked up the guts to introduce yourself to the neighbor, it's time to say good-bye.

Probably the hardest transitional sacrifices are the friendships. Finding friends is hard. Making friends even harder. Many relationships require time, and time isn't always on your side.

But it's important to stay by your husband's side during these transitions. After God, he is your primary and most important relationship.

I always wondered why God made woman from the rib of a man until I realized the location of the rib is at the man's side. He wants husbands and wives to stand side by side through all the difficulties and struggles of life.

You are not *following* your husband to the next location, carrying his boxes and golf bag. You are standing side by side, holding hands and supporting each other along the way.

Jesus knew the difficulties of relocation. His parents moved from Nazareth to Bethlehem, then to Egypt, then back to Nazareth—all of this before Jesus learned to walk! When Jesus started his ministry, he had no mailing address, roaming around Israel from place to place. Then after his thirty-three-year stint on earth, Jesus packed up his bags and transferred back to heaven. His disciples didn't want him to leave, so he reminded them that they wouldn't be alone: "Nevertheless I tell you the truth. It is to your advantage that I go away; for if I do not go away, the Helper will not come to you; but if I depart, I will send Him to you" (John 16:7 NKJV).

Counselor means many things, such as "friend" or "helper," two people you need the most when you move into unfamiliar territory. Although he won't help you pack boxes or move the piano to the fourth floor, he will come alongside you, fill you with peace, and move in your heart as never before.

The Counselor, the Friend, the Helper, is the Holy Spirit. You can find just as much Holy Spirit in Tulsa as you can in Tallahassee. He works in Bangor and Bangkok. His address reads everywhere from Atlanta to Zanzibar . . . and from heaven to earth.

Jesus took his spiritual family with him everywhere he went. And so should you.

God never sends you out alone. When everything in life changes, one thing cannot: the Holy Spirit will always be at your side.

108.

SO OFTEN I WANT TO SAY ENCOURAGING WORDS TO MY HUSBAND, BUT I GET NERVOUS AND FIGURE HE WON'T CARE ANYWAY. DOES IT MATTER WHETHER I SPEAK UP OR NOT?

In many houses discouragement is the language everyone speaks. The home is a war zone, and the warriors have nicknames like Stupid, Idiot, Dummy, and Little Pain in the Neck. Bullets and shrapnel litter their lives. Blood splatters on the walls. They live with scars and treat their open wounds.

In other homes, families follow the spirit of the Western tune "Home on the Range." There, a discouraging word is seldom heard. People hide their hurts with smiles on their faces. Maybe the reason discouragement is seldom heard is because words are seldom heard. Silence is deadly.

Other homes flourish with encouragement. Everyone believes in one another, supports one another, edifies, refreshes. Pats on the back. Notes in their lunch boxes. Love letters under the pillows. Hearts expressed. Prayers.

Which home would you rather live in?

You may be the first person to rebuild the encouragement foundation of your house, but it's a positive first step. Remodel now, and pick the new pattern of speaking that will decorate your home forever. Remove the weeds, and allow the sweet-smelling flowers of love to bloom.

When you talk, do not say harmful things, but say what people need—words that will help others become stronger. (Eph. 4:29 NCV)

109.

WHEN JESUS PRESENTED HARDNESS OF HEARTS AS THE REASON FOR DIVORCE (MATT. 19:8), WHAT DID HE MEAN?

Romance begins with soft hearts. Hand holding. Cuddling. We have pet names for each other. We apologize, take the blame, and share the chores. But let a few years pass, a few babies come, and cardiac calcification sets in.

There is a disagreement. He sits on one side of the couch and she on the other. He's thinking, *I'm not going to apologize. Not me.* She's thinking, *If he believes I'm going to admit my mistake, he's smoking something.*

This is a crossroads moment. Will one take the high road and honor the vow? Or will both love pride more than the other person and grumble, "I'm going to make this hurt"? Sometimes one of the two hearts softens. But one is not enough. Marriage depends on two tender hearts.

Hard hearts can't support a marriage. Eventually one of the hard-hearted spouses meets a kind associate or neighbor, and adultery knocks on the door. To prevent this, God builds a moat around the home. "I hate divorce!" he announced (Mal. 2:16 NLT). It hurts children. It makes a mockery out of marriage. It breaks the backbone of society. God hates divorce.

But God loves his children. And he knows there is a hard-hearted streak in all of us. So what does God do? How does he accommodate the hard-heartedness of people? Destroy them with lightning? Wink and look away as if to say, "Everyone messes up"?

No, he protects the tenderhearted. And he makes it possible for the hardhearted to repent and start over.

Mark it down, however: Divorce is not his will. A tenderhearted marriage is.

110.

MY HUSBAND HAS ADMITTED TO HAVING AN AFFAIR. WE'VE STRUGGLED FOR YEARS TO KEEP OUR LOVELESS MARRIAGE ALIVE. ALL MY FRIENDS TELL ME I SHOULD DIVORCE HIM WHILE I'M YOUNG ENOUGH TO MARRY AGAIN. SHOULD I LISTEN TO THEM? DIVORCE SEEMS LIKE SUCH A DRASTIC STEP, AND I KNOW IT WOULD HURT OUR KIDS.

When two become one, as the Bible describes marriage, they join together with an invisible bonding agent so adhesive that, when broken, it splinters. Marriage is not held together with spit and polish so that it slides apart easily when the two people go their separate ways. Divorce shatters that bond and the lives of the people involved.

Hearts break. Plans disintegrate. Pieces of trust lie all over the place. And it's not just the spouses who must put their lives back together but the children, the aunts and uncles, the grandparents, the friends. Divorce is a nuclear bomb that wipes out everything in its path.

So should you seek a divorce? No. It's never the first option.

Go back to those vows, the moment that first brought you together. Remember the motivation that caused you to say those words. You promised to stay together no matter what, even if you don't feel in love.

Love is not a feeling. Love is a commitment. Thankfully, God does not love me based on whether he feels I meet all his standards. He loves me because he promised to love me in sickness and in health, for better and worse, for as long as we both shall live (which is eternally).

And God always keeps his word. May he help us keep ours.

111.

I'VE FALLEN IN LOVE WITH A DIVORCED MAN WHO HAS TWO CHILDREN. I'VE NEVER BEEN MARRIED, SO I WONDER WHETHER GOD LOOKS WITH ANY DISFAVOR ON MARRIAGES TO DIVORCED PEOPLE. CAN YOU HELP ME WITH THESE CONCERNS?

Jesus was asked about divorce and remarriage.

> The Pharisees also came to Him, testing Him, and saying to Him, "Is it lawful for a man to divorce his wife for just any reason?"
>
> And He answered and said to them, "Have you not read that He who made them at the beginning 'made them male and female,' and said, 'For this reason a man shall leave his father and mother and be joined to his wife, and the two shall become one flesh'? So then, they are no longer two but one flesh. Therefore what God has joined together, let not man separate."
>
> They said to Him, "Why then did Moses command to give a certificate of divorce, and to put her away?"
>
> He said to them, "Moses, because of the hardness of your hearts, permitted you to divorce your wives, but from the beginning it was not so. And I say to you, whoever divorces his wife, except for sexual immorality, and marries another, commits adultery; and whoever marries her who is divorced commits adultery." (Matt. 19:3–9 NKJV)

Our society plays musical chairs with marriages, exchanging lovers like partners at a square dance. God says stay put and stay faithful.

The home is sacred and should be guarded like a fortress. Only one thing, in Jesus' eyes, warrants divorce—an ongoing choice by one partner to be sexually active with a person outside the marriage.

Divorce should never be taken lightly. If reconciliation is absolutely you'll-be-talking-to-my-lawyers impossible, then what else can you do? If every means of repairing the relationship has been tried, tested, and tossed out, what's Plan B?

So does God forgive those who get divorced? How about an adulterer? Can the unfaithful ever again have a happy marriage?

God forgave King David. For David, adultery became a lifestyle, with all those wives and concubine girlfriends. He satisfied his own desires yet broke God's desire for marriage. David even committed murder to get Bathsheba. So does God forgive murderers and adulterers? Thieves on a cross? Persecutors on the road to Damascus? All the time.

God forgives, but he prefers to prevent. Forgiven people can move on with their lives, but they must deal with the consequences of their choice and all the hurt that accompanies it.

Since divorce is inevitable in this world, God can certainly bless two forgiving and forgiven hearts who desire to start over and make it right the second time.

Home

Diapers, Disagreements,
and "Any hope for prodigals?"

Dear Will –

Your questions and concerns
over your prodigal daughter
must surely weigh heavily
on you. As a father, I
can only imagine your
heartache, helplessness, and
desire for reunion. May
God give you the comfort
no human can. Don't stop
praying for your child. God
always hears the prayers of
a parent.

Max

112. What should I tell my kids about sex?

When we became parents, we took on the roles of chauffeur, chaperone, EMT, coach, provider, recreational director, and sex education instructor. Most of us feel woefully inadequate on this last assignment. However, some ideas may help.

Model healthy sexuality in your home. Express appropriate affection. When kids see parents holding hands or kissing good-bye before going to work, this sends a healthy message: physical affection is not to be feared.

On the other hand, if children discover inappropriate sexuality in the lives of their parents, the poor example leaves an indelible impression. If children find their dad's porn on the computer or in the garage, discover romantic text messages on mom's phone but not sent by dad, or awaken to see their single parent's date from the night before cooking breakfast, they take note. Hypocrisy speaks loudly. Don't underestimate the damage of a bad example, and don't underestimate the power of a good one.

Be "askable." When we hear our kids ask about condoms, periods, or intercourse, we are tempted to cover our ears or wash out their mouths. There is no need to overreact. Just do your best. Give clear, age-appropriate answers. Small children need only basic information. Teenagers need more details. At some point all children need to understand that sexual activity and desires are God's good idea. Urgings and interests are not dirty or dangerous. Sex is God's gift, yet it is a wedding gift.

Again, children deserve to hear this message from their parents. I like the idea of parents presenting their child, sometime in early adolescence, with a purity ring or necklace that the teenager can wear as a symbol. Others cosign covenants of sexual purity in which parents and kids promise to honor God's standard.

Connect with a community of faith. You stack the odds in your children's favor by plugging them into a Christian youth group. This only makes sense. When teenagers' best friends are Christians, when their favorite hangout is a youth group, when you help them have healthy peers and hear Christ-honoring truth, you're giving your children a head start.

Make your home a place of grace. Young people mess up. They go too far too fast, and when they do, moms and dads, let's give them a safe place to land. Let's give our children what God gives us: clear teaching, appropriate correction, and abundant forgiveness.

113.

I GREW UP IN A HOME WITH NO DISCIPLINE. MY PARENTS LET ME DO ANYTHING I WANTED TO DO, AND I DID. IN RAISING MY KIDS, I DON'T WANT TO FOLLOW THEIR EXAMPLE. I DON'T WANT TO OVER-DISCIPLINE EITHER. WHAT IS THE BALANCE?

Gardeners know how to straighten a tree. Some saplings are strong and healthy but are headed in the wrong direction. They suffer from a lean. Wanting the tree to grow straight, what does the gardener do? He ties a rope to the trunk, straightens the tree, and stakes the rope into the ground. Henceforth, as the tree grows, it is pulled in the right direction.

Children need the same correctional tug. The Bible calls this *discipline*.

> Folly is bound up in the heart of a child,
> > but the rod of discipline will drive it far from him. (Prov. 22:15)

> A refusal to correct is a refusal to love;
> > love your children by disciplining them. (Prov. 13:24 MSG)

Scripture never endorses physical abuse or irresponsible chastening. The Bible does teach that punishment is a deterrent for defiant disobedience. In fact, under the Law of Moses, rebelling against parents was a capital offense (Deut. 21:18–21). There's no mention in history of its ever being used, but for sure it was threatened!

Discipline is not easy, but these principles helped Denalyn and me.

Be careful. Be quick to interrupt misbehavior but slow to punish it. Place a child in time-out while you both cool down. Punishment is never a license for cruelty. If you are enjoying the administration of the discipline, you need to stop.

Be consistent. The punishment must fit the act. Seek to discern the cause of the action. What motivated this behavior? It's one thing to slam a door out of disrespect. It's another to slam it because the ice cream truck is on the street. Forgetting to clean the room is one matter; stomping a foot and refusing to clean it is another. Oversights are misdemeanors. Rebellion is a felony.

Be clear. Explain what the punishment is and what the offense was. Do not assume the child understands. Do not punish a child for "being bad." The child may have done a bad thing, but that doesn't mean he is a bad child.

Be compassionate. One mistake does not a child make. One season of waywardness does not a child define. "Love does not keep a record of wrongs" (1 Cor. 13:5 TEV). But love does keep a list of things done well.

114.
MY WIFE AND I SERVE ON A FOREIGN MISSION FIELD. WE MOVED OUR FAMILY HERE IN RESPONSE TO GOD'S GUIDANCE. BUT NOW WE ARE FACING PROBLEMS WITH OUR KIDS, AND WE ARE WONDERING WHETHER WE MADE A MISTAKE IN COMING HERE.

I wonder how Noah felt, cramming his family onto a luxury animal cruise (Gen. 6:13–7:5).

Did Abraham ever regret moving from Ur to Canaan (Gen. 12:1–4)?

Or did Joseph question his forced relocation into slavery (Gen. 37:12–28)?

I wonder if Moses ever thought that moving his family and his people to the promised land was a mistake (Genesis–Deuteronomy).

I'm sure at times all of them suffered a twinge of doubt, but overall, in the end, it made sense. Why? Because God called all of them to these places.

Hebrews 11 summarizes the stories of people who were asked to do things by God, but none of the tasks made sense at the time. They acted in faith. The kind of faith that does but never sees.

If God called you to a foreign mission field, he already knows all the parameters, all the possibilities, all the problems that could occur. He's considered what will happen to you and your spouse, how it will affect your kids, and what it will mean to the people you serve.

He took care of Noah, Abraham, Joseph, Moses, and their families as they moved out into foreign mission fields.

Why not you?

115.
EVERY DAY I WORRY ABOUT MY CHILDREN. ALTHOUGH THEY ARE SAFE AND HAPPY TODAY, I STILL WORRY ABOUT THEM. I WORRY IF THEY WILL REMAIN TRUE TO GOD. I WORRY IF THEY WILL MARRY GOOD PEOPLE. I WORRY IF THEY MIGHT GET SICK AND SUFFER PAIN. HOW DO I CONTROL THESE WORRIES?

What would parents do without worry? It almost seems as if it's in the job description: "Parents Wanted. Must be able to perform sleepless nights and meaningless pacing, wringing their hands and biting their nails."

The only things worry promises are stubby fingers and sore feet.

Can all your worries add a single moment to your life? (Matt. 6:27 NLT)

Worry has no positive side effects. In fact, it subtracts moments from your life in the form of heart stress and rising blood pressure.

Worry is antitrust. If you are worried, you don't trust something.

~ Your kids	~ The weather
~ Their mode of transportation	~ The church
~ Their friends	~ Their future spouse
~ Strangers	~ God

God takes care of millions of birds, billions of flowers. Can he take care of your children? Certainly.

How do you stop worrying? Jesus made it clear.

Therefore I tell you, stop being perpetually uneasy (anxious and worried) about your life. (Matt. 6:25 AMPLIFIED BIBLE)

Pretty blunt answer. Stop it! Just say no to worry. Slap at it like a bloodsucking mosquito. Easier said than done, huh?

Worry tests your trust, so hand your children to God and let him babysit your babies when you're not around. He's pretty good at it.

Casting the whole of your care [all your anxieties, all your worries, all your concerns, once and for all] on Him. (1 Peter 5:7 AMPLIFIED BIBLE)

116.
OUR LITTLE BOY SUFFERS WITH A CRIPPLING DISEASE. IT BREAKS MY HEART TO SEE HIM SUFFER PHYSICAL PAIN, BUT IT HURTS EVEN MORE WHEN HE SUFFERS PAIN FROM REJECTION AND HURTFUL WORDS FROM OTHER CHILDREN. SOMETIMES I CAN BARELY BREATHE BECAUSE MY HEART HURTS SO MUCH. HOW CAN I KEEP HIS SUFFERING IN PERSPECTIVE?

To keep your son's suffering in perspective, remember:

God himself is a father. What parental emotion has he not felt? Are you separated from your child? So was God. Is someone mistreating your child? They mocked and bullied his. Is someone taking advantage of your child? The Son of God was set up by false testimony and betrayed by a greedy follower. Are you forced to watch while your child suffers? God watched his Son on the cross.

In addition, we are God's children, suffering in a world of sin that wreaks havoc on our bodies, twists our minds, and severs our relationships. Does God shrug his shoulders and say, "Oh well, that's life"? Of course not. Why would he go to all the trouble of introducing himself to the world with the title of Father? Curator, Manager, and Overseer are colder titles of indifference. God's role is not a job. It's a relationship. So God chose a relationship title you can identify with. Now you understand his heart when his children are in pain.

So whatever emotions you feel about your son, God feels about your son. Maybe more. I know that's hard to believe, but God has known your son longer than you have. He hurt for him before he was born. You're not alone. Your Father weeps right by your side.

God is your son's Father too. Just as you'll do everything to help your son during his pain, so will God.

117.
NOW THAT MY TWO SONS ARE ADULTS, THEY HAVE STRAYED FAR FROM GOD. I PRAY DAILY FOR THEIR RETURN. AS I WAIT, I CAN'T HELP BUT WORRY THAT THEIR HEARTS ARE BECOMING HARDER AND THAT THEY WILL NOT RETURN TO GOD.

No child of God is too far from home.

The prodigal son assumed he was. He had spurned his father's kindness and "journeyed to a far country, and there wasted his possessions with prodigal living" (Luke 15:13 NKJV). The word translated here as *wasted* is the same Greek verb used to describe the action of a seed-sowing farmer. Envision him throwing handfuls of seeds onto tilled earth. Envision the prodigal tossing his father's money to greedy merchants: a roll of bills at one club, a handful of coins at another. He rides the magic carpet of cash from one party to the next. His heart grows hard.

And then one day his wallet grows thin. The credit card comes back. The maître d' says, "No;" the hotel says, "Go;" and the boy says, "Uh-oh." He slides from high hog at the trough to low pig in the mud. He finds employment feeding swine. Not a recommended career path for a Jewish boy. His heart breaks.

The hunger so gnaws at his gut that he considers eating with the pigs. But rather than swallow the pods, he swallows his pride and begins that famous walk homeward, rehearsing a repentance speech with each step. Turns out he didn't need it. "His father saw him and had compassion, and ran and fell on his neck and kissed him" (v. 20 NKJV). The father was saving the son's place. His heart softened.

There's a place for your sons too. They are always invited to return to the place of honor. It just takes some time and some prayer to get their hearts right.

118.

FOR YEARS I'VE STRUGGLED TO GET ALONG WITH MY MOTHER-IN-LAW. SHE IS VERY CRITICAL AND NOT AN EASY PERSON TO LOVE, BUT I FEEL LIKE I'VE JUST DEVELOPED A HABIT OF DISLIKING HER. DO YOU REALLY THINK I CAN CHANGE MY ATTITUDE TOWARD HER?

Ah, the mother-in-law. For years she has been the target of so many jokes. Just saying "my mother-in-law" gets a chuckle every time. "Oh yeah," the giggler responds, "the mother-in-law!" (I wonder if in mother-in-law circles they laugh when they hear the expression "the son-in-law.")

Sometimes it's true. Mothers-in-law can be hard to get along with. And when you're at odds with your own mother-in-law, it's no laughing matter. You can't change her, but you can change the way you see her.

Here are three practical steps.

Focus: In order to change my attitude toward someone, I change my focus. I stop looking at the thing that drives me up the wall and instead search through the nooks and crannies of his personality for a quality worthy of my attention.

Your focus is on your mother-in-law's negativity, but what's her best quality? Is she generous? A great cook? An excellent people person? I ask God, "What do you love about this person?" He always finds something.

Past: Somewhere along the way I discover why a person acts the way he does—what his childhood was like, who hurt him, what failures ripple through his life—and I empathize with him, feeling sorry for the hand life dealt him.

Pray: Finally, I pray for the person. It's hard to stand before God and speak horribly about someone whom you know God loves.

These steps may not change your mother-in-law, but they will help change your attitude toward her. And who knows, maybe she'll start to change when you start to see her differently.

119. MORE THAN ANYTHING IN THE WORLD I WANT TO BE A GOOD MOM TO MY KIDS. HOW CAN I BE THE MOM GOD WANTS ME TO BE?

The virgin birth is more, much more, than a Christmas story. It is a picture of how close Christ will come to you, a mom, as you also bring a child into the world.

Imagine yourself in that story found in Luke 1.

God comes to you and says, "I have a special task for you. A child. A special child that I want to entrust to you. Are you willing to raise this one?"

You stammer, take a breath. "This sounds scary."

"Don't worry. I'll be there with you. This child is special to me. He will be a great child."

You shake your head. "Such an awesome responsibility. I don't know if I can do it."

"Nothing is impossible with me."

You smile. "I am your servant. I'll do it."

Do we think only one child received God's special attention? Sure, only one was his Son, and an angel sent out those special birth announcements, accompanied by an angelic choir singing "Happy Birthday." Of course God pulled out all the stops for Jesus' birth.

But children aren't randomly born to parents. God orchestrates the right children to be born to the right parents.

Being the mom God wants you to be starts with the understanding of how important your job is in God's eyes. He entrusts you with one of his own children. He chose you out of all the moms in the world for this one child.

Remember, you, too, are highly favored by God himself to receive such a special gift.

120.

Some folks don't know we have an option. To listen to our vocabulary, you'd think we are the victims of our thoughts. "Don't talk to me," we say. "I'm in a bad mood." As if a mood were a place to which we are assigned ("I can't call you; I'm in Bosnia") rather than an emotion we permit.

Or we say, "Don't mess with her. She has a bad disposition." Is a disposition something we "have"? Like a cold or the flu? Are we the victims of the emotional bacteria of the season? Or do we have a choice?

Paul says we do: "We capture every thought and make it give up and obey Christ" (2 Cor. 10:5 NCV).

Do you hear some battlefield jargon in that passage—"capture every thought," "make it give up and obey Christ"? You get the impression that we are the soldiers and the thoughts are our enemies. Our assignment is to protect the homeland and refuse entrance to trashy thoughts. The minute they appear on the horizon, we go into action. "This heart belongs to God," we declare, "and you aren't getting in here until you change your allegiance."

"Selfishness, step back! Envy, get lost! Find another home, Anger! You aren't allowed on this turf." Capturing thoughts is serious business.

We are not a victim of our thoughts. We have a vote. We have a voice. We can exercise thought prevention.

121.

MY JOB REQUIRES LOTS OF OVERTIME, SO I CAN'T ATTEND MANY OF MY KIDS' SCHOOL ACTIVITIES. MY WIFE WORRIES ABOUT THIS A LOT. COULD THIS HAVE A NEGATIVE EFFECT ON OUR KIDS? OR ON MY RELATIONSHIP WITH THEM?

As a father of three girls, I struggled with the same issues. As God blessed my ministry, more and more calls came in from all over the world, wanting me to speak at churches, conferences, and grand openings of supermarkets. It was hard to say no at first. I felt every opportunity was from God.

Finally I realized that every time I said yes to something, I had to say no to something else. It's called Max's Yes Law of Inverse Dynamics. *Look it up!* It says this: with every yes in your schedule, there is an equal and opposite no reaction.

When I said yes to another speaking engagement, I said no to another family dinner.

When I said yes to another meeting, I said no to my girls' volleyball game.

When I said yes to another book tour, I said no to taking a walk with my wife.

So how do we show people that we love and believe in them? There are many ways to express those feelings—verbal affirmations, love letters, phone calls, even a quick text message saying, "I'm thinking of you." They're all good, but there's one that's the best.

I talked about it in my book *A Love Worth Giving*:

Do you believe in your kids? Then show up. Show up at their games. Show up at their plays. Show up at their recitals. It may not be possible to make each one, but it's sure worth the effort . . . You want to bring out the best in someone? Then show up.

Now that my girls are all grown up, believe me, I'm glad I made that decision to show up before it was too late. Now (cue "Cat's in the Cradle" in the background) I miss those Meet the Teacher Nights and seeing their papier-mâché volcano at the science fair and sitting in the stands at the big volleyball meet, even if they were on the bench the whole time.

When it comes to kids and family, it is a lot easier to make money than to make up lost time.

122.
THE WORLD TODAY—PEOPLE AND CERTAINLY THE MEDIA— ENCOURAGES OUR CHILDREN TO BE SELF-INDULGENT. I DON'T THINK ALL THIS SELF-PREOCCUPATION WILL HELP THEM GROW INTO MATURE ADULTS. AM I OFF BASE HERE?

Taught at an early age, self-indulgence becomes a way of life. Every beat of a child's heart becomes "me-me, me-me, me-me, me-me."

Television does not present the best models:

- ~ Kids who get every gadget and goody they want
- ~ Kids who, in thirty minutes, solve all their problems
- ~ Kids who get laughs with their sassy comebacks to stupid adults

Television dangles the fruit in front of our kids and says, "Doesn't this way of life look good? Indulge yourself."

But self-indulgence is a problem facing not only our children but humankind. In fact, self-indulgence got us into this mess. "Go ahead, Eve. Eat that fruit. It looks so good. Indulge yourself."

Television only promotes what the world already thinks. So how do you teach your children well? Give them new models.

Other kids—Make sure they hang out with other kids who don't "have it all" or whose parents don't rush out and buy the latest thing.

Parents—Are they learning self-indulgence from you? Do your schedule and your own priorities take precedence over them? Do you have more toys than they do?

Jesus—Feed them a consistent message of Jesus Christ, focusing on his humility and his self-sacrifice. "Jesus . . . was given a position 'a little lower than the angels'" (Heb. 2:9 NLT). Jesus chose servanthood, and he is the King! Can't we do the same?

Kids need to get turned on to new models of self-sacrifice to realize that life is not one big TV show and the plots don't always center on them.

123. WE'RE TRYING TO TEACH OUR CHILDREN HUMILITY, BUT AT THE SAME TIME WE DON'T WANT TO DESTROY THEIR SELF-ESTEEM. WHAT WOULD YOU SAY IS A GOOD BALANCE?

There are two verses, both found in Philippians, that you should teach your kids because they balance the spectrum of humility and self-esteem.

> Do nothing out of selfish ambition or vain conceit, but in humility consider others better than yourselves. (2:3)

> I can do everything through him [God] who gives me strength. (4:13)

Philippians 2:3 says to treat others better than myself.
Philippians 4:13 says God treats me well.
The first says others are more worthy than I am.
The second says I am worthy because God uses me.
The first says I am lower than others.
The second says I am greater because of God's strength.

Self-esteem is what people see when they look in the mirror—what they understand as their value. A constant diet of "you're not important; others are" certainly seems to devalue a person. But it doesn't have to, as long as you remember the second verse. You are strong.

One characteristic we don't find in Jesus is a lack of confidence. He took on the Pharisees, braved angry crowds, stood his ground when others twisted his words, went to the cross confident of his mission, and all the while "did not come to be served, but to serve, and to give his life as a ransom for many" (Mark 10:45).

Teach your child to be a confident servant who knows his purpose in serving others and loves his boss because his boss loved him first and gives him all the strength he needs to face the world.

124.

WE TAUGHT OUR KIDS THE BIBLE, BUT THEY HAVE LEFT GOD. WHAT HAPPENED? WE THOUGHT IF WE TRAINED THEM IN GOD'S WORD, THEY WOULD NOT DEPART FROM HIM. ISN'T THAT WHAT THE BIBLE SAYS?

> Train up a child in the way he should go,
> And when he is old he will not depart from it. (Prov. 22:6 NKJV)

Be careful with this verse. Don't interpret it to mean "If I put my kids on the right path, they'll never leave it. If I fill them full of Scripture and Bible lessons and sermons, they may rebel, but they'll eventually return."

The proverb makes no such promise. Salvation is a work of God. Godly parents can prepare the soil and sow the seed, but God gives the growth (1 Cor. 3:6). Moms and dads soften hearts but can't control them.

Show them the path? Yes.

Force them to take it? No.

At moments in my own life I stood at the crossroads of the path and even took a few steps down the wrong one. One thing always brought me back—that inner compass shown to me by my Christ-loving parents.

No child ever leaves God's sight. A child may turn his back on God or try to hide from his sight. But leave God's view? Impossible. God has his eye on every child of his.

The Holy Spirit will follow your child down every back road, every dark alley, every dead end and always remind him of the foundation of belief you showed him—the road back home.

My wife shares this verse with the parents of prodigals. It is a good one for you: "The LORD says, 'This is my agreement with these people: My Spirit and my words that I give you will never leave you or your children or your grandchildren, now and forever'" (Is. 59:21 NCV).

125.
I was raised in a Christian home, but now that I'm thirty-four and unmarried, I struggle with loneliness and insecurity. I'm afraid of being alone but even more afraid of the temptation to embrace sin just to keep from being alone. Where can I find a candle of hope in the darkness of loneliness?

It's natural that you long for companionship. It's in our DNA. God used part of a man to make a woman. A couple fits together like a human puzzle, strengths complementing weaknesses, passions unifying hearts, love at the core. These two undefined pieces make a complete picture when they meet. Consequently, a single person might feel incomplete. Life becomes an unfinished puzzle for them, searching for the other piece.

Many singles think marriage makes life perfect. Hmm, just ask a married person about that. Marriage complicates many things. Being single, at times, is easier. You have only one person to worry about. Add a spouse and a couple of kids, and your needs become secondary.

Paul knew this and liked being single.

> I would like you to be free from concern. An unmarried man is concerned about the Lord's affairs—how he can please the Lord. But a married man is concerned about the affairs of this world—how he can please his wife—and his interests are divided. An unmarried woman or virgin is concerned about the Lord's affairs: Her aim is to be devoted to the Lord in both body and spirit. But a married woman is concerned about the affairs of this world—how she can please her husband. I am saying this for your own good, not to restrict you, but that you may live in a right way in undivided devotion to the Lord. (1 Cor. 7:32–35)

Marriage redefines our service. Participating in Bible studies and working at the homeless shelter are replaced with family dinners and our spouses' office parties. For many of us, this is great.

Paul, however, felt that marriage would divide his attention.

As a single man, Paul traveled all over Asia and Europe, spreading the gospel. He started churches and debated some of the smartest scholars of all time. What about Peter? What did Peter do? Peter was married. Jesus healed his mother-in-law, which means Peter had a wife (Matt. 8:14–15). At the beginning of Acts, we hear a lot about Peter and his work in and around Israel. Yet we don't hear of Peter's adventures around the world. Why? He probably had to stay home, near his wife and family. He took three years off to travel with Christ, but after that, his ministry area became more confined because his attention was divided.

Was Peter ineffective? No. Was he limited in his effectiveness? Yes. Marriage limited him.

Paul goes on to say, "Look, if you can't restrain yourself, get married" (see 1 Cor. 7:9). But don't miss the heart of the teaching: unmarrieds may be without a spouse, but they are not without a groom. Singles can be a vital part of the bride of Christ, the church, as it prepares itself for that final, great wedding day.

126. OUR FAMILY ISSUE IS MONEY. MY HUSBAND AND I CAN'T AGREE ON HOW MUCH TO SPEND, SAVE, OR GIVE.

Denalyn and I had to sort this one out as well. We were raised in two different environments. My parents were very frugal and debt resistant. They never took out a loan or spent a penny they didn't record. Denalyn's parents were more spontaneous and credit dependent. Consequently, when we married, I wanted to save more, and Denalyn wanted to spend more.

We had to spend some time learning what the Bible says about money. According to Scripture, God gives you a paycheck for four reasons.

To honor your God: "Honor the Lord with your wealth and with the best part of everything you produce" (Prov. 3:9 NLT). Your checkbook is an instrument of worship. Just as you honor God with your voice and your prayer, you honor God when you give money to his work.

To provide for your family: "But those who won't care for their relatives, especially those in their own household, have denied the true faith. Such people are worse than unbelievers" (1 Tim. 5:8 NLT). These are some of the hardest words in the Bible. God never intended for children to go hungry or families to suffer in the cold. The well-being of the family trumps the need for bass boats or diamonds every time.

To support your country: "Pay your taxes and government fees to those who collect them, and give respect and honor to those who are in authority" (Rom. 13:7 NLT). Roads must be paid for. Schools must be supported. Citizens of heaven are not exempt from doing their share on earth.

To enjoy it: "Teach those who are rich in this world not to be proud and not to trust in their money, which is so unreliable. Their trust should be in God, who richly gives us all we need for our enjoyment" (1 Tim. 6:17 NLT).

These four priorities helped Denalyn and me map out a simple strategy for money management. In our second year of marriage, after too many tense moments about money, we came up with this plan:

10 percent to the church
10 percent to savings
80 percent to bills and fun

We both felt the conviction to tithe. I felt the conviction to save, and Denalyn felt led to encourage free enterprise. So we compromised. After we have honored

God and put some money in savings, the 80 percent that remains has always been sufficient for day-to-day needs. This plan has worked so well for us that we've been able to increase giving well beyond the 10 percent level.

Find a plan that works for you.

127.
I REALLY DREAD GOING HOME FOR THE HOLIDAYS. MY PARENTS AND BROTHERS TURN CHRISTMAS INTO CHAOS. THEY DON'T RESPECT ME OR ENCOURAGE ME. IN FACT, THEY HARDLY TALK TO ME.

We can't control the way our family responds to us. When it comes to the behavior of others toward us, our hands are tied. We have to move beyond the naive expectation that if we do good, people will treat us right. The fact is, they may, or they may not.

If your father is a jerk, you could be the world's best daughter, and he still wouldn't tell you so.

If your aunt doesn't like your career, you could change jobs a dozen times and still never satisfy her.

If your sister is always complaining about what you got and she didn't, you could give her everything, and she still might not change.

As long as you think you can control people's behavior toward you, you are held in bondage by their opinions. If you think you can control their opinion and their opinion isn't positive, then guess whom you have to blame. Yourself.

It's a game with unfair rules and fatal finishes.

I can't assure you that your family will ever give you the blessing you seek, but I know God will. Let God give you what your family doesn't. If your earthly father doesn't affirm you, then let your heavenly Father take his place.

How do you do that? By emotionally accepting God as your Father. You see, it's one thing to accept him as Lord, another to recognize him as Savior, but it's another matter entirely to accept him as Father.

God has proven himself as a faithful Father. Now it falls to us to be trusting children. Let God give you what your family doesn't. Let him fill the void others have left. Rely on him for your affirmation and encouragement. Look at Paul's words: "You are God's child, and *God will give you the blessing he promised*, because you are his child" (Gal. 4:7 NCV, emphasis mine).

128.
OUR FAMILY IS EXHAUSTED. WE RUN FROM ONE EVENT TO THE NEXT. HOW DO WE SLOW DOWN?

Jesus understands. He knew the frenzy of life. People back-to-backed his calendar with demands. But he also knew how to step away from the game.

> Now when it was day, He departed and went into a deserted place. (Luke 4:42 NKJV)

Jesus placed the mob in the rearview mirror and ducked into a wildlife preserve, a hidden cove, a vacant building, a *deserted place*. Later in the verse Luke identifies the reason: "the crowd . . . tried to keep Him from leaving them." People brought Jesus more than sick bodies and seeking souls. They brought him agendas. Itineraries. Unsolicited advice. The herd of humanity wanted to set Jesus' course. "Heed us," they said. "We'll direct your steps."

They say the same to you. Look over your shoulder, my friend. The crowd is one step back. Moreover, they seem to know more about your life than you do. Where you should work. Whom you should marry. What you should study. They will lead your life if you allow them.

Jesus didn't. Follow his example.

Deserted need not mean desolate, just quiet. Simply a place to which you, like Jesus, *depart*. "Now when it was day, He departed." *Depart* presupposes a decision on the part of Jesus. "I need to get away. To think. To ponder. To rechart my course." He determined the time, selected a place. With resolve, he pressed the pause button on his life.

God rested after six days of work, and the world didn't collapse. What makes us think it will if we do? (Or do we fear it won't?)

129. I HAVE ONE CHILD IN MIDDLE SCHOOL AND ANOTHER STARTING TO DRIVE. AM I WRONG TO WORRY ABOUT THEM?

No, you are a parent. And Jesus heeds the concern in a parent's heart. After all, our kids were his kids first. "Don't you see that children are God's best gift? the fruit of the womb his generous legacy?" (Ps. 127:3 MSG). Before they were ours, they were his. Even as they are ours, they are still his.

We tend to forget this fact, regarding our children as *our* children as though we have the final say in their health and welfare. We don't. All people are God's people, including the small people who sit at our tables. Wise are the parents who regularly give their children back to God.

Jesus said so little about parenting, made no comments about spanking, breast-feeding, sibling rivalry, or schooling. Yet his actions spoke volumes about prayer. Each time a parent prayed, Christ responded. His big message to moms and dads? Bring your children to me. Raise them in a greenhouse of prayer.

When you send them off for the day, do so with a blessing. When you tell them good night, cover them in prayer. Is your daughter stumped by geography homework? Pray with her about it. Is your son intimidated by the new girl? Pray with him about her. Pray that your children have a profound sense of place in this world and a heavenly place in the next.

God never dismisses a parent's prayer.

130.

My husband and I want to be hospitable, but our house is small, and I'm a lousy cook, so I hesitate to invite people over. My husband says these things don't matter as much as being hospitable. Is he right?

Your husband is right. The event need not be elaborate to be significant. Don't listen to the Martha Stewart voice that says everything must be perfect. The house must be perfect. The china must be perfect. Meal. Kids. Husband. Scented guest towels, warm appetizers, after-dinner mints. Everything must be perfect.

If we wait until everything is perfect, we'll never issue an invitation.

It's no accident that *hospitality* and *hospital* come from the same Latin word, for they both lead to the same result: healing. When you open your door to someone, you are sending this message: "You matter to me and to God." You may think you are saying, "Come over for a visit." But what your guest hears is, "I'm worth the effort."

Do you know people who need this message? Singles who eat alone? Young couples who are far from home? Seniors who no longer drive? Some people pass an entire day with no meaningful contact with anyone else. Your hospitality can be their hospital. All you need are a few basic practices.

Issue a genuine invitation. Let your guests know you want them to come. Call them on the phone, or step over to their desks at work. People weather so many daily rejections. The doctor can't see them. The kids didn't call. The airplane is booked. But then you invite them over. *We have room for you!* Life altering.

Make a big deal of their arrival. Gather the entire family at the front door. Swing it open as you see them approach. If you have a driveway, meet them on it. If your apartment complex has a lobby, be waiting for them. This is a parade-worthy moment. One of God's children is coming to your house!

Address the needs of your guests. First-century hospitality included footwashing. Modern-day hospitality includes the sharing of food and drink. Time to talk and listen. No televisions blaring in the background. No invasive music.

Send them out with a blessing. Make it clear you are glad your guests came. Offer a prayer for their safety and a word of encouragement for their travel.

Remember this: what is common to you is a banquet to someone else. You think your house is small, but to the lonely heart, it is a castle. You think the living room is a mess, but to the person whose life is a mess, your house is a sanctuary. You think the meal is simple, but to those who eat alone every night, pork and beans on paper plates tastes like filet mignon. What is small to you is huge to them.

131. I'VE PUT MY FAMILY IN A DANGEROUS FINANCIAL BIND BECAUSE OF MY MISTAKES. I'M TOO PROUD TO ASK FOR HELP, BUT ON THE OTHER HAND I AM SCARED OF RUINING MY MARRIAGE AND MY FAMILY.

Two fears are operating simultaneously here:

1. the fear of destroying a marriage and a family
2. the fear of destroying your reputation

The first fear is hard to reconcile since it involves many different people with different needs. Families are delicate. One false move and the whole thing could go to pieces. So many opinions, pasts, and regrets. Families are very complicated.

The second fear involves only you. Asking for help, you believe, cries of weakness. You feel you'll lose respect and your standing in the community.

In the first fear, you are motivated by your love for your family.

In the second, you are motivated by your love of yourself.

Which do you think God cares more about—your family or your reputation?

Pride is a stubborn, sticky mess of self-preservation. God never, ever approves of it.

Admitting you are weak is admitting the truth. We all are weak. We all need help. We all need God. We can't save ourselves. It's the entire theme of the Bible. When humans try to help themselves, it only causes more problems.

Get help for your finances before you need to get help for your family. Putting your well-being aside for the sake of others is the stuff heroes are made of.

132.
MY PARENTS ARE GREAT CHRISTIANS, BUT THEY WANT TO CONTROL MY LIFE. THEY FEEL THEY SHOULD BE INVOLVED IN MAKING THE DECISIONS ABOUT WHOM I MARRY, WHERE I GO TO COLLEGE, AND WHAT CAREER I PURSUE. I WANT TO HONOR MY PARENTS, BUT WHAT IF I FEEL THEIR IDEAS CONFLICT WITH GOD'S WILL FOR MY LIFE?

I am a son and a parent, so I see both sides of your conflict.

As a son, I, too, wanted to be set free, released into the world to leave my mark, to show everyone my value, and to make my own decisions about my future.

As a parent, I understand fearing that our children will make the wrong decisions, loving them so much that I still want to rock them in my arms, and longing to protect them from the mean ol' world.

It's easy to know if your parents' ideas conflict with God's will for your life. Ask yourself these two questions:

1. Are they contrary to God's Word?
2. Do they run counter to your passions?

Your parents have known you longer than you've consciously known yourself. Their ideas may be worth considering.

That feeling of conflict may be pride—stubbornly holding your *me* ground and not wanting anyone to tell you what to do. You don't have to do what they suggest, but you should at least listen to them and consider it. If they are Christians, they should be taking signals from the same God you follow. He may be speaking through them.

Honor your mother and father by consulting them and considering their counsel. Honor God by following his will for your life. As Christians, your parents should understand.

Haves/
Have-Nots

Work, Money,
and "Where's the lifeline?"

MAX LUCADO

Ellen—

Your financial struggles have
not gone unnoticed in
heaven. Though God hasn't
given you the answers
you've yearned for, that
doesn't mean he's not acting
on your behalf. Instead of
dollars, God may be provid-
ing an opportunity to know
and trust him more. You
have a choice: either deny
God and turn away, or trust.
Please choose trust —

Max

133.
I HAVE ONE OF THE MOST UNGLAMOROUS JOBS IN THE WORLD.
I CLEAN HOTEL ROOMS. SOME PEOPLE LOOK DOWN THEIR
NOSES AT SUCH A LOW-LEVEL JOB. SO DOES MY WORK MATTER TO GOD?
OR IS IT MERELY A WAY TO PAY MY BILLS AND BUY THE GROCERIES?

God has ordained your work as something good. Before he gave Adam a wife or a child, even before he gave Adam britches, God gave Adam a job. "Then the LORD God took the man and put him into the garden of Eden to cultivate it and keep it" (Gen. 2:15 NASB).

God views work worthy of its own engraved commandment: "You shall work six days, but on the seventh day you shall rest" (Ex. 34:21 NASB). We like the second half of that verse and work for the weekend. But emphasis on the day of rest might cause us to miss the command to work: "You shall work six days." Whether you work at home or in the marketplace, your work matters to God.

And your work matters to society. We need you! Cities need plumbers. Nations need soldiers. Stoplights break. Bones break. We need people to repair the first and set the second. Someone has to raise kids, raise cane, and manage the kids who raise Cain.

Whether you log on or lace up for the day, you imitate God. Jehovah himself worked for the first six days of creation. Jesus said, "My Father never stops working, and so I keep working, too" (John 5:17 NCV). Your career consumes half of your lifetime. Shouldn't it broadcast God? Don't those forty to sixty hours a week belong to him as well?

The Bible never promotes workaholism or an addiction to employment for pain medication. But God calls all the physically able to till the gardens he gives. God honors work. So honor God in your work.

And whatever you do, whether in word or deed, do it all in the name of the Lord Jesus, giving thanks to God the Father through him. (Col. 3:17)

Do you know what the phrase "whatever you do" means in Greek?

Whatever you do! So whatever you do, do it as if Jesus is stamping his name on your time card, or signing off on the work, or autographing your project.

Then give thanks to God for your job, for the provision, for the opportunity to share his love with the world . . .

No matter what you do.

134.
My wife and I have piled up a small (make that a huge) mountain of debt. We're always shopping for the latest gadgets and new clothes. How can we get off of this credit-card roller coaster?

Lean in closer. Closer. I want to whisper to you the solution to overspending. That's it. Put the book up to your ear.

Stop spending so much!!

Sorry, didn't mean to scream at you. Just wanted to make sure you heard that.

Is that solution too simple? It's not. Spending reveals some attitudes we have about ourselves, our security, and our God.

If your back had a kink in it, I would say see a chiropractor and get a spinal readjustment.

If your finances are out of whack, I would say talk to God and get a financial readjustment.

Here are two biblical truths that can do that.

> Naked a man comes from his mother's womb,
>   and as he comes, so he departs.
> He takes nothing from his labor
>   that he can carry in his hand. (Eccl. 5:15)

We entered this world naked. Ask any maternity-ward nurse. We leave this world in a box, wearing only a suit or a dress. Ask any funeral-home director. While caskets may contain memorabilia, we can't take our money or cars or homes with us. When we die, we say bye-bye to what we buy.

> [Jesus said,] "Life is not defined by what you have, even when you have a lot."
> (Luke 12:15 MSG)

You are not your credit-card statement. What you buy may reflect aspects of your personality. The purchases may explain you, but they don't define you.

Your heart is who you are. "The LORD does not look at the things man looks at. Man looks at the outward appearance, but the LORD looks at the heart" (1 Sam. 16:7). God doesn't see you driving a German-built car, wearing an Italian silk suit, and playing with the latest gadget from Silicon Valley. When God thinks of you, he sees your compassion, your devotion, your tenderness . . . your heart.

If you define yourself by your stuff, you'll feel good when you have a lot and bad when you don't.

With these two biblical principles in mind, you should hear a tension-releasing crack in your financial spine, allowing you to walk tall and erect with the burden of debt off your back.

135. MY FATHER IS A DOCTOR. MY GRANDFATHER IS A DOCTOR. EVERYONE EXPECTS ME TO BE A DOCTOR. I WANT TO STUDY MUSIC. DID I MISS SOMETHING?

No, I think you found something. People often say, "You can be anything you want to be. Be a butcher if you want to, a sales rep if you like. Be an ambassador if you really care. You can be anything you want to be—if you work hard enough."

But can you? If God didn't pack within you the meat sense of a butcher, the people skills of a salesperson, or the world vision of an ambassador, can you be one? An unhappy, dissatisfied one perhaps. But a fulfilled one? No. Can an acorn become a rose, a whale fly like a bird, or lead become gold? Absolutely not.

You cannot be anything you want to be. But you can be everything God wants you to be.

God never prefabs or mass-produces people. No slapdash shaping. "I make all things new," he declares (Rev. 21:5 NKJV). He didn't hand you your granddad's bag or your aunt's life; he personally and deliberately packed you.

Live out of the bag God gave you. Enjoy making music.

136. THIS YEAR HAS HAD NOTHING BUT TURMOIL FOR ME. I WORK IN MANUFACTURING; WE'VE TAKEN A BIG HIT IN THIS ECONOMIC DOWNTURN, AND EVERY DAY I FEAR LOSING MY JOB. HOW CAN I BE LESS FEARFUL ABOUT THIS SITUATION?

When employment drops and the Dow Jones hits rock bottom and the economy plunges into recession, the Bible makes it clear:

Look up!

The apostle Paul wrote, "Command those who are rich in this present world not to be arrogant nor to put their hope in wealth, which is so uncertain" (1 Tim. 6:17).

When you gaze at your income, your investments, and your job, you watch a wild, unpredictable roller coaster racing out of control. Up and down. Up and down. It gets dizzying, nauseating, straining every muscle in our bodies, sometimes so severely that we get serious kinks in our necks.

In fact, the Bible says people who refuse to look up to God are stiff-necked (Jer. 17:23). Their necks refuse to pivot skyward and gaze at God. Life has caused them to pull a faith muscle. Now they're stuck looking straight ahead, or down, at their own path and their own way.

When you look to God, it's quite a different story, because your hope is placed in the One who owns all the riches, who knows the future and establishes kingdoms.

Next time you catch yourself gazing at your riches, look at the back of the dollar bill. It clearly reads "In God We Trust."

Not always the case for us.

For many of us, it's "In Money We Trust."

"In Defense Systems We Trust."

"In Man We Trust."

"In Jobs We Trust."

"In Myself I Trust."

The Bible realigns our necks.

> Some trust in chariots and some in horses,
> but we trust in the name of the LORD our God. (Ps. 20:7)

In God, whose word I praise,

in God I trust; I will not be afraid.

What can mortal man do to me? (Ps. 56:4)

Do not let your hearts be troubled. Trust in God; trust also in me. (John 14:1)

Stop looking left and right, forward and back. That's the workout of a paranoid, fearful person. Just look up and trust God with your finances.

137.

THE COMPANY I WORKED AT FOR MORE THAN FORTY YEARS FORCED ME TO TAKE EARLY RETIREMENT. THIS MADE ME FEEL AS IF MY LIFE IS OVER FOR GOOD. BUT I STILL HAVE GREAT HEALTH AND ENERGY. DO YOU THINK GOD CAN STILL USE ME, OR AM I TOO OLD?

To the angel of the church in Philadelphia write:

These are the words of him who is holy and true, who holds the key of David. What he opens no one can shut, and what he shuts no one can open. I know your deeds. See, I have placed before you an open door that no one can shut. I know that you have little strength, yet you have kept my word and have not denied my name. (Rev. 3:7–8)

Jesus is a doorman. He opens and shuts doors all the time, and no one can close what he has opened, and no one can open what he has closed. He stands at doors and knocks (Rev. 3:20). If they are locked, he has a key. If he doesn't want to use the key, he walks through the walls (John 20:19). But better than being just a doorman, Jesus is the door (John 10:9 NCV)!

So what is Jesus trying to say with all this talk about doors? He controls all gateways and passages from one place to another. Nothing gets past him without his knowing it.

Jesus doesn't leave us standing in the hallway or outside in the cold. He has something for us—new opportunities, new destinations, new chances to show our faith in him.

What do we do as we wait for other doors to open? In the book of Revelation, Jesus makes it clear to the church of Philadelphia—keep God's Word and commands, stay faithful, and don't curse or deny him.

Right now Jesus is sorting through that vast key ring, looking for the right door for you. He may have to lock and unlock a few other doors first, but one is sure to open soon.

Trust him. It's an open-and-shut case.

138.

SUCH PRESSURE IS BEING PLACED ON OUR KIDS TO CHOOSE A VOCATION THAT WILL GIVE THEM MATERIAL BENEFITS. THEY NOT ONLY GET THIS MESSAGE FROM OUR CULTURE BUT ALSO FROM OUR FAMILY. THEY HEAR IT FROM THEIR GRANDPARENTS! HOW CAN WE HELP THEM SEE THE DANGER IN GREED?

In 1900, the average person living in the United States wanted seventy-two different things and considered eighteen of them essential. Today the average person wants five hundred things and considers one hundred of them essential.[1]

Our obsession with stuff carries a hefty price tag. We spend 110 percent of our disposable income trying to manage debt.[2] And who can keep up? We no longer measure ourselves against the Joneses next door but against the star on the screen or the stud on the magazine cover. Hollywood's diamonds make yours look like a gumball-machine toy. Who can satisfy Madison Avenue? No one can. For that reason Jesus warns, "Be on your guard against every form of greed" (Luke 12:15 NASB).

Greed comes in many forms. Greed for approval. Greed for applause. Greed for status. Greed for the best office, the fastest car, the prettiest date. Greed has many faces but speaks one language: the language of more. Wise was the one who wrote, "Whoever loves money never has money enough; whoever loves wealth is never satisfied with his income" (Eccl. 5:10).

Greed can never be satisfied. It will always want more. It will never have enough. It cries "Feed me" all day and all night. Greed is always hungry.

Parents need to teach their children about greed before it swallows them whole. The only way to feel full is to feel fulfilled. The only way to feel fulfilled is to understand that everything we have comes from God and he gives us exactly what we need. All of it is on loan, and someday we will have to give it all back, checking it in at heaven's door.

139.

THINGS ARE GETTING REALLY DICEY AT WORK. WITH ALL THE LAYOFFS, MY COLLEAGUES ARE REDEFINING INTEGRITY. SOME ARE CLAIMING SALES THEY DID NOT MAKE. OTHERS ARE PADDING THEIR EXPENSE ACCOUNTS. I EMPATHIZE WITH THEIR ACTIONS. IN FACT, I'M TEMPTED TO HEDGE MY BETS A BIT MYSELF.

Be careful. Don't make a decision in a storm that you wouldn't make in calm weather.

I have a friend who recently learned to fly. His teacher wanted to train him to trust the instrument panel because storms and fog can distort the perspective of the pilot. He may think he is flying safely when actually he is descending toward the earth.

To prove his point, the teacher took my friend up and blocked his view so he had to rely on the panel. The teacher then rocked and rolled the plane so much that the student was dizzy, and his equilibrium was off. The teacher then turned over the controls to his pupil. My friend was convinced he had leveled out the plane. His instinct, his impression was that the flight was flat. The instrument panel told another story. According to the controls, he was descending toward the earth.

Now, what should he trust?

The same happens to us. Circumstances and struggles bounce us around. Our perspective gets distorted and our equilibrium out of whack. In those hours we have to make decisions. Do we commit adultery? Or remain faithful? Do we cheat? Or stay honest? Do we compromise? Or take a stand?

Can we trust our instincts in the storm? The Bible says we can't. "There is a way that seems right to a man, but its end is the way of death" (Prov. 14:12 NKJV).

In the rough and tumble of bad weather, we need an outside force. We need a guide that is unaffected by storms. Don't listen to your friends. Listen to your Father.

140.

MY HUSBAND HAD A HIGH-PAYING JOB THAT ALLOWED US TO HAVE A COMFORTABLE LIFESTYLE. HIS POSITION WAS TERMINATED LAST YEAR, AND HE HAD TO TAKE A MAJOR SALARY CUT. WE'VE MOVED TO A SMALLER HOUSE, AND OUR BUDGET IS SUPERTIGHT NOW. I'M HAVING A HARD TIME ACCEPTING THESE CHANGES, AND THEY ARE CAUSING STRIFE IN OUR MARRIAGE.

We, like Paul, must learn the "secret of being happy at any time in everything that happens, when I have enough to eat and when I go hungry, when I have more than I need and when I do not have enough. I can do all things through Christ, because he gives me strength" (Phil. 4:12–13 NCV).

What is the secret of being happy at any time . . . in everything?

Whether we're well fed or starving to death?

When we have more and when we have less?

The secret is—get ready—Christ, who gives us strength.

Paul does not say "the Christ who gives me money."

Or "the Christ who fills my bank account."

Or "the Christ who makes everything come out the way I want."

He just gives us strength—the strength to be courageous, generous, resourceful, kind, thoughtful, humble, frugal, and loving, no matter what happens.

What do we really need when we run head-on into life's walls? The strength to get up. Not our strength. We just got knocked out cold! But the strength that comes from God's helping hand getting us back on our feet.

What do we really need when we've walked months and years across life's hills and valleys? The strength to go on. Not our strength. We're worn-out!

When everything has been taken from you, God's strength is the only thing left. Good thing. It's the one thing we really need.

141.

WE RECENTLY LOST QUITE A BIT OF MONEY IN THE STOCK MARKET, AND MY HUSBAND HAS BECOME SO PARANOID ABOUT OUR FINANCIAL CONDITION THAT HE TALKS ABOUT IT CONSTANTLY AND HAS BECOME A TIGHTWAD. IT SEEMS LIKE HE'S GOING OVERBOARD. HOW CAN I HELP HIM REGAIN SOME BALANCE?

Balancing between risk and obsession requires wisdom.

Being thrifty when you're facing economic uncertainty is wise. You need to tap the brakes around slippery slopes and tighten the belt around gluttonous appetites.

Do you know what the balance is between penny-pincher and big spender? Generosity.

Penny-pincher brings to mind Charles Dickens's Scrooge.

Big spender conjures up images of Dudley Moore's Arthur.

Notice the extremes. One hoards money. The other wastes.

Both of them do it for the same reason—selfishness. By not spending they protect themselves. "It's all mine. I'll keep it if I want to!"

By overspending, they reward themselves. "It's all mine. I'll spend it if I want to!"

So if selfishness defines the extremes, then generosity determines the balance.

Instead of spending or not spending on yourself, spend it on others. Give. God blesses a cheerful giver (2 Cor. 9:7). Nowhere in Scripture will you find God blessing a stingy miser or an egotistical millionaire.

Don't worry about where to spend the next dollar on yourself. Figure out places you can give together.

Like you, many others are struggling and need help. There's no better time to give and to bring balance to your economic situation.

142. MY OFFICE WALL IS COVERED WITH MY AWARDS AND DIPLOMAS. A CLIENT RECENTLY MADE A NEGATIVE COMMENT ABOUT THEM, QUESTIONING MY HUMILITY. IS HE RIGHT?

I suppose you could take them down, unless you did so out of pride. Humility is a tricky thing. If you think you have it, you probably don't. Here are some ideas about humility.

Assess yourself honestly. "Don't cherish exaggerated ideas of yourself or your importance, but try to have a sane estimate of your capabilities by the light of the faith that God has given to you" (Rom. 12:3 PHILLIPS).

Don't take success too seriously. "When your . . . silver and gold increase . . . your heart will become proud" (Deut. 8:13–14).

Celebrate the significance of others. "In humility consider others better than yourselves" (Phil. 2:3).

Don't demand your own parking place. "Go sit in a seat that is not important" (Luke 14:10 NCV).

Never announce your success before it occurs. "One who puts on his armor should not boast like one who takes it off" (1 Kings 20:11).

Speak humbly. "Let no arrogance come from your mouth" (1 Sam. 2:3 NKJV).

Live at the foot of the cross. "The cross of our Lord Jesus Christ is my only reason for bragging" (Gal. 6:14 NCV).

If you really want to remember great accomplishments, place a cross on your wall.

143.
MY HUSBAND AND I ARE MAKING MORE MONEY THAN EVER. WE'VE SEEN SUCCESS RUIN PEOPLE AND WANT TO BE CAREFUL TO AVOID THEIR MISTAKES.

Good for you. Make this your theme verse:

> Command those who are rich in this present age not to be haughty, nor to trust in uncertain riches but in the living God, who gives us richly all things to enjoy. Let them do good, that they be rich in good works, ready to give, willing to share, storing up for themselves a good foundation for the time to come, that they may lay hold on eternal life. (1 Tim. 6:17–19 NKJV)

Do not be haughty. Do not think for a moment that you had anything to do with your accumulation. Scripture makes this clear: Your stocks, cash, and 401(k)? They are not yours.

> To the LORD your God belong the heavens, even the highest heavens, the earth and everything in it. (Deut. 10:14)

> Yours, O LORD, is the greatness and the power
>   and the glory and the majesty and the splendor,
>   for everything in heaven and earth is yours. (1 Chron. 29:11)

> "The silver is mine and the gold is mine," declares the LORD Almighty. (Hag. 2:8)

Do not put your "trust in uncertain riches." Or as one translation reads, "[the rich] must not be haughty nor set their hopes on riches—that unstable foundation" (1 Tim. 6:17 WEYMOUTH). Money is an untrustworthy foundation.

God owns everything and gives us all things to enjoy. Less hoarding, more sharing. "Do good . . . be rich in good works, ready to give, willing to share."

144. I WAS BORN TO WORRY. WHAT ADVICE DO YOU HAVE FOR US FRETTERS?

Pray, first. Inoculate yourself inwardly to face your fears outwardly. "Casting the whole of your care [all your anxieties, all your worries, all your concerns, once and for all] on Him." (1 Peter 5:7 AMPLIFIED BIBLE).

Easy, now. Slow down. "Rest in the LORD, and wait patiently for Him" (Ps. 37:7 NKJV). Assess the problem. Take it to Jesus and state it clearly.

Act on it. The moment a concern surfaces, deal with it. Don't dwell on it. Don't waste an hour wondering what your boss thinks; ask her. Before you diagnose that mole as cancer, have it examined. Be a doer, not a stewer.

Compile a worry list. Over a period of days, record your anxious thoughts. Maintain a list of all the things that trouble you. How many of them turned into a reality?

Evaluate your worry categories. Your list will highlight themes of worry. Pray specifically about them.

Focus on today. God meets daily needs daily. Not weekly or annually. He will give you what you need when you need it. "Let us therefore boldly approach the throne of our gracious God, where we may receive mercy and in his grace find *timely* help" (Heb. 4:16 NEB, emphasis mine).

Unleash a worry army. Share your feelings with a few loved ones. Ask them to pray with and for you.

Let God be enough. Jesus concludes his call to calmness with this challenge: "Your heavenly Father already knows all your needs. Seek the Kingdom of God above all else, and live righteously, and he will give you everything you need" (Matt. 6:32–33 NLT).

P-E-A-C-E. It is possible with God.

145.
IN MOST OF MY PRAYERS I ASK GOD FOR THINGS I NEED EACH DAY. THESE ARE LEGITIMATE NEEDS. (I'M NOT ASKING GOD TO MAKE ME A MILLIONAIRE, JUST TO HELP ME PAY THE MORTGAGE.) IS GOD REALLY CONCERNED ABOUT THE NECESSITIES OF MY LIFE?

"Give us each day our daily bread" (Luke 11:3).

What is this daily bread Jesus spoke of, tucked inside the Lord's Prayer? A loaf of warm Italian bread on my doorstep every morning? That would be nice.

Bread is a staple of every culture. From flat bread to yeast-filled loaves, grain has been mixed with water and oil and placed over a fire by every civilization. What's the first thing a restaurant brings before the meal? Bread. (Okay, maybe Mexican restaurants don't, but those chips are made from grain. They're just fried in oil.)

But how about a slight change to the daily menu: "Give us this day our daily mocha chocolate chip ice cream" or "Give us this day our daily beluga whale caviar"?

Those are luxuries, not necessities. Sorry, God does not promise those.

Bread is a valued necessity, tasty and welcomed, but certainly not extravagant.

Jesus tells us to ask for the necessities in life, but does he promise to provide them?

Soon after this plea for daily bread, found also in Matthew 6, Jesus presents his famous "Don't worry" passage: "Therefore I tell you, do not worry about your life, what you will eat or drink; or about your body, what you will wear. Is not life more important than food, and the body more important than clothes?" (v. 25). God takes care of birds, flowers, and grass and provides the basics they need to exist (vv. 26–30). Why not us? Aren't we more important than a barn swallow, a multiflora petunia, and a blade of Bahia grass?

You bet a loaf of sweet sourdough we are.

In that statement comes a promise from God to provide his most important creation on earth with food, clothing, and drink (vv. 25–34). The necessities once again.

Jesus tells us to ask, then promises to give us the basics we need to survive.

So don't worry; be prayerful. God has something wonderful for us baking in the oven. Can you smell it?

146.

I'D LIKE TO SLOW DOWN AND SIMPLIFY MY LIFE. MY WIFE AND I WORK MANY HOURS EACH WEEK AND HAVE LESS AND LESS TIME AT HOME. IT'S JUST THAT WE ARE BOTH SO AMBITIOUS.

Are you ambitious? Or are you discontent?

Think for just a moment about the things you own. Think about the house you have, the car you drive, the money you've saved. Think about the jewelry you've inherited and the stocks you've traded and the clothes you've purchased. Envision all your stuff, and let me remind you:

You don't get to keep it.

Here is a healthy exercise. Affix a sticky note to everything in your life that is going to burn up. Spend time walking around your house, office, yard, and garage, and stick a Post-it to all things destined for destruction: your car, your desk, your savings account, your house. What is going to be destroyed when Christ comes?

Once you've finished, step back and look around. What's left? Your spouse. Your kids. Your friends. Your church. The Word of God. Most notably, your soul. "And what do you benefit if you gain the whole world but lose your own soul? Is anything worth more than your soul?" (Matt. 16:26 NLT). Doesn't it make sense to invest in things of eternity? All that stuff you have now? You don't get to keep it.

In fact, *you never had it.* You own nothing. You are simply a steward of what God has given you. "The earth is the LORD's, and everything in it. The world and all its people belong to him" (Ps. 24:1 NLT).

Your stuff is not yours. Ever since you grabbed that toy and yelled, "Mine!" you've been lying. Everything is God's. So keep money in perspective.

Years ago I came across this proverb, which has since gone through several variations: Money can buy you a bed but not sleep. Books but not knowledge. Food but not an appetite. Finery but not beauty. A house but not a home. Medicine but not health. Pleasures but not peace. Luxuries but not life. Amusements but not joy. A church building but not a church. A crucifix but not a cross. Stuff but not a Savior.

147.

I'VE WORKED SIXTY-HOUR WEEKS FOR THE PAST YEAR TO BUILD UP MY OWN BUSINESS, BUT NOW I'M BURNED-OUT. I'M GROUCHY, EVEN WHEN I'M WITH MY FAMILY, AND I FEEL DEPRESSED. HOW CAN I REJUVENATE MY LIFE WITHOUT LOSING MY BUSINESS?

What do you do when you run out of gas?

Stare at the gauge? Blame your upbringing? Deny the problem? Never works.

In the case of an empty tank, we've learned: get the car to a gas pump ASAP. In life, we try to push the car ourselves. We are in such a hurry to get to where we want to go that we scoff at the service station, get out of the driver's seat, and try to do things with our own effort. Push, push, push. Stopping for gas is for wimps.

If you are putting in sixty hours a week to build up your "own" business, that tells me you are pushing the car yourself. And you're getting very tired.

Sounds as though you may be suffering from a fuel-less faith. You need to fill yourself with some high-test fuel. Remember Phillips 66, a once-popular gas station? Try some Philippians 6—six promises from a premium-grade book:

Being confident of this, that he who began a good work in you will carry it on to completion until the day of Christ Jesus. (1:6)

For to me, to live is Christ and to die is gain. (1:21)

Do nothing out of selfish ambition or vain conceit, but in humility consider others better than yourselves. (2:3)

I want to know Christ and the power of his resurrection and the fellowship of sharing in his sufferings, becoming like him in his death. (3:10)

I press on toward the goal to win the prize for which God has called me heavenward in Christ Jesus. (3:14)

I can do everything through him who gives me strength. (4:13)

Fill your tank with verses like these, and stop trying to push yourself around. God is able to do what you can't.

Hereafter

Cemeteries, Heaven, Hell,
and "Who goes where?"

MAX LUCADO

Charles —

I'm happy to tell you that you don't have to go to hell. Jesus died so you could be saved and spend eternity with Him. Ask Him to forgive your sins and be your Savior. <u>He will</u>! Find a church where you can be baptized, learn about the Bible, and grow in your faith.

Stay Strong!

Max

148.
THE SEVEN-YEAR-OLD SON OF OUR NEIGHBORS DIED LAST WEEK. THEY ARE DEVASTATED. SO ARE WE. WHAT CAN WE TELL THEM?

God is a good God. We must begin here. Though we don't understand his actions, we can trust his heart.

God does only what is good. But how can death be good? Some mourners don't ask this question. When the quantity of years has outstripped the quality of years, we don't ask how death can be good.

But the father of the dead teenager does. The widow of the young soldier does. The parents of a seven-year-old do. How could death be good?

Part of the answer may be found in Isaiah 57:1–2: "Good people are taken away, but no one understands. Those who do right are being taken away from evil and are given peace. Those who live as God wants find rest in death" (NCV).

Death is God's way of taking people away from evil. From what kind of evil? An extended disease? An addiction? A dark season of rebellion? We don't know. But we know that no person lives one day more or less than God intends. "All the days planned for me were written in your book before I was one day old" (Ps. 139:16 NCV).

But her days here were so few . . .

His life was so brief . . .

To us it seems that way. We speak of a short life, but compared to eternity, who has a long one? A person's days on earth may appear as a drop in the ocean. Yours and mine may seem like a thimbleful. But compared to the Pacific of eternity, even the years of Methuselah filled no more than a glass. James was not speaking just to the young when he said, "Your life is like a mist. You can see it for a short time, but then it goes away" (James 4:14 NCV).

In God's plan every life is long enough and every death is timely. And though you and I might wish for a longer life, God knows better.

And—this is important—though you and I may wish a longer life for our loved ones, they don't. Ironically, the first to accept God's decision of death is the one who dies.

While we are shaking heads in disbelief, they are lifting hands in worship. While we are mourning at a grave, they are marveling at heaven. While we are questioning God, they are praising God.

149.

Because you buried more than a person. You buried some of yourself. Wasn't it John Donne who said, "Any man's death diminishes me"? It's as if the human race resides on a huge trampoline. The movements of one can be felt by all. And the closer the relationship, the more profound the exit. When someone you love dies, it affects you.

It affects your dreams.

Some years ago my wife and I served with other missionaries in Rio de Janeiro, Brazil. Our team consisted of several young couples who, by virtue of being far away from home, became very close. We rejoiced greatly when two of our team members, Marty and Angela, announced that she was pregnant with their first child.

The pregnancy was difficult, however, and the joy became concern. Angela was told to stay in bed, and we were urged to stay in prayer. We did. And the Lord answered our prayers, though not as we desired. The baby died in the womb.

I've never forgotten Marty's comment: "More than a baby died, Max. A dream died."

Why does grief linger? Because you are dealing with more than memories; you are dealing with unlived tomorrows. You're not just battling sorrow; you're battling disappointment. You're also battling anger.

It may be on the surface. It may be subterranean. It may be a flame. It may be a blowtorch. But anger lives in sorrow's house. Anger at self. Anger at life. Anger at the military or the hospital or the highway system. But most of all, anger at God. Anger that takes the form of the three-letter question—why? Why him? Why her? Why now? Why us?

You and I both know I can't answer that question. Only God knows the reasons behind his actions. Keep giving yourself time. Grieve at your own pace. At the right time the sorrow will pass.

Egyptians may dress in black for six months. Muslims wear mourning clothes for a year. Orthodox Jews offer prayers for a deceased parent every day for eleven months. Just fifty years ago rural Americans wore black armbands for several weeks.[1] And today? Am I the only one who senses that we hurry our hurts?

Grief takes time. Give yourself some. "Sages invest themselves in hurt and grieving" (Eccl. 7:4 msg). The son of David wrote, "Sorrow is better than laughter, for sadness has a refining influence on us" (Eccl. 7:3 nlt).

150.

WE HEAR THAT THERE IS LIFE AFTER DEATH, BUT HOW CAN WE BE SURE? HOW CAN WE BE SURE WE WILL LIVE AGAIN? SOME PEOPLE THINK WE WILL JUST SLEEP FOREVER AFTER DEATH.

How can we be sure there is life after death?

The Bible says so. "Because Jesus was raised from the dead, we've been given a brand-new life and have everything to live for, including a future in heaven—and the future starts now!" (1 Peter 1:3–4 MSG).

Jesus said so. "This is what is written: The Christ will suffer and rise from the dead on the third day, and repentance and forgiveness of sins will be preached in his name to all nations, beginning at Jerusalem. You are witnesses of these things" (Luke 24:46–48).

The angel said so. "Do not be afraid, for I know that you are looking for Jesus, who was crucified. He is not here; he has risen, just as he said. Come and see the place where he lay" (Matt. 28:5–6).

Witnesses said so. "He was seen by Peter and then by the twelve apostles. After that, Jesus was seen by more than five hundred of the believers at the same time" (1 Cor. 15:5–6 NCV).

Even the rolled-away stone testifies to Christ's rising from the dead (Matt. 28:1–7). No barrier will keep us locked inside the grave. Christ was the first example that we will all follow.

While we wait for this glorious resurrection, what are our spirits doing? Jesus spoke of death as sleep when talking to the disciples about Lazarus:

After he had said this, he went on to tell them, "Our friend Lazarus has fallen asleep; but I am going there to wake him up."

His disciples replied, "Lord, if he sleeps, he will get better." Jesus had been speaking of his death, but his disciples thought he meant natural sleep. (John 11:11–13)

Is death a time of unconscious, REM-driven snoozing? In the story of the rich man and Lazarus (a different Lazarus) in Luke 16, Jesus described a conscious death with an awareness of events, people, and identity. So it can't be sound-asleep sleep.

When we are asleep, our bodies transition into a different state, just like death. Still, motionless, the body lies there, yet the brain keeps working in an altered state of consciousness. In death, consciousness also shifts as the spirit leaves the body behind. The body waits for its own moment at the resurrection when it will be stirred awake by the alarm clock call of the final trumpet and rise anew from its tomb to be reunited with its still-conscious spirit and the Person who conquered death before us all.

151. A DEAR CHRISTIAN FRIEND OF OURS RECENTLY DIED IN A CAR ACCIDENT. THIS HAS BEEN ESPECIALLY HARD FOR HIS WIFE OF FORTY YEARS. SHE IS A BELIEVER, TOO, BUT SHE WONDERS AND WORRIES ABOUT WHETHER SHE WILL TRULY SEE HIM AGAIN. CAN YOU GIVE ME SOME WORDS OF COMFORT TO SHARE WITH HER?

God has the last word on death. And, if you listen, he will tell you the truth about your loved ones. They've been dismissed from the hospital called Earth. You and I still roam the halls, smell the medicines, and eat green beans and Jell-O off plastic trays. They, meanwhile, enjoy picnics, inhale springtime, and run through knee-high flowers. You miss them like crazy, but can you deny the truth?

They have no pain, doubt, or struggle. They really are happier in heaven.

And won't you see them soon? Life rushes by at mach speed. "You have made my days a mere handbreadth; the span of my years is as nothing before you. Each man's life is but a breath" (Ps. 39:5).

When you drop off your kids at school, do you weep as though you'll never see them again? When you drop off your spouse at the store and park the car, do you bid a final forever farewell? No. When you say, "I'll see you soon," you mean it. When you stand in the cemetery and stare down at the soft, freshly turned earth and promise, "I'll see you soon," you speak truth. Reunion is a splinter of an eternal moment away.

There is no need for you "to grieve like the rest of men, who have no hope" (1 Thess. 4:13). So go ahead, face your grief. Give yourself time. Permit yourself tears. God understands. He knows the sorrow of a grave. He buried his Son. But he also knows the joy of resurrection. And by his power, you will too.

152.
MY HUSBAND AND I SUFFERED WITH INFERTILITY FOR FIVE YEARS. WE WERE SO HAPPY LAST YEAR WHEN WE FINALLY HAD A BEAUTIFUL BABY GIRL, BUT SHE LIVED ONLY TWO MONTHS. THE LOSS OF OUR DAUGHTER IS ALMOST MORE THAN I CAN BEAR. MY ARMS LONG TO HOLD MY BABY. HOW DO I LIVE WITH THIS GRIEF?

Society tells us one way to deal with grief.

"Don't cry."

"Keep a stiff upper lip."

"Stay strong."

Our hearts send us a different message.

"Let it all out."

"Have a good cry."

The Bible agrees with our hearts. When I read the Scriptures, I see all kinds of emotions prompted by hurt and pain. David cried out to God. Jesus wept at the death of Lazarus. There's a whole book called Lamentations. Seventy percent of Psalms speaks of sorrows.

Grieving is a release valve of emotions. So feel free. It's okay.

Don't put pressure on yourself to get better too soon. You don't have to snap out of it until you're ready. Death is a shock to the system, flipping your world upside down. A vital part of your life has been stripped from you, and you need time to reorient to a new way of living—to refocus your goals and dream new dreams.

Solomon explained, "There is . . . a time to mourn" (Eccl. 3:1, 4). Life faces its winter seasons, but every winter is followed by a spring. Paul urged the Thessalonians to grieve, but he didn't want the Christians to "carry on over them like people who have nothing to look forward to, as if the grave were the last word" (1 Thess. 4:13 MSG).

Finally, never forget . . . there is hope. The grave wins battles, but it will never win the war. As the women at the tomb and the apostles grieving in the Upper Room discovered, someday all our tears will be dried, our hurt will turn to joy as we are reunited in heaven with those we lost on earth, and death will finally become a distant memory of the past (Matt. 28:8–9; John 20:19–20).

153.

My grandmother is dying of a rare blood disorder. She suffers a lot, and I think it would be merciful for her to die, as she is ready to meet Jesus. But my mother wants me to pray that God will keep Grandma alive. How do we know the right way to pray in situations like this?

> All the days planned for me
>> were written in your book
>> before I was one day old. (Ps. 139:16 NCV)

We all have a start date and an end date, known by God before we were born. The clock began ticking the moment we were conceived in the womb.

Life and death are (thankfully) not for us to determine. Why? We cannot see what would happen if we lived a day longer or a day shorter. God can see all of that and determines the best time for our funeral. Who knows what could happen if your loved one died on a Wednesday or a Friday instead of a Thursday? It's too much for us to ponder. Too many variables and questions we can't answer.

> Your life is like a mist. You can see it for a short time, but then it goes away. (James 4:14 NCV)

Life is never too long or too short. Then again, it's never long enough as we say good-bye to loved ones and never short enough when we watch them suffer.

On this side of the grave, death is so final and so difficult.

A time is coming, though, when death will be tossed into the garbage. Revelation 20:14 says death and the grave will be things of the past and thrown into the incinerator. Yesterday's news. We won't think about the concept of death any longer. Do you think about the trash you threw out last week? That's the way death will be.

Your grandmother will stand with us in heaven, alive and well. Death does not shorten our lives. It transports us to the next.

154.
I'VE BEEN READING A BOOK ABOUT THE AFTERLIFE, AND I WONDER WHAT OUR RESURRECTED BODIES WILL BE LIKE. I'VE STRUGGLED FOR YEARS WITH A WEIGHT PROBLEM, SO I SURE HOPE I HAVE A DIFFERENT BODY IN HEAVEN!

I love to trade in my old car and get a new one. That new-car smell. The quiet ride. The clean interior. All those stains gone. No more mysterious rattles. No more worn tires.

When we die and Jesus resurrects our bodies, we will get a bodily trade-in. The old clunkers will be gone, and the latest models will roll out.

"He will take these dying bodies of ours and change them into glorious bodies like his own" (Phil. 3:21 TLB). Jesus, at the resurrection, displayed for us the promised resurrected body we will one day receive.

This is a promise not of a different make but of a new model. Brand-new. Clean. Stain free. No loose parts. No wear and tear. It will be designed for eternity and run at its optimal capacity. Plus, it comes with a lifetime guarantee.

That means your eyes will always work as they're supposed to. No more glasses.

Your legs will be the exact same length. No more corrective shoes.

Your tongue will form words properly. No more stuttering.

Your spine will be perfectly aligned. No more crutches.

Your metabolism will burn calories at the rate it was designed to. No more weight problems.

Will we have scars? Jesus keeps his, but they act as a praise reminder of what he did for us on the cross. Our scars speak of the horrors and evil of this world. We won't take them with us.

We were not designed to be mentally unstable, crippled, or blind. In fact, when Jesus found people who were handicapped, he healed them. Why? Handicaps were not part of God's original plan. If the man born blind was meant to be blind, Jesus would have left him that way.

We will all be the optimal size we need to be. Maybe short people will be a little taller and tall people a little shorter. Maybe skinny people will be a little heavier. Changes occur in our blueprints because of an imperfect genetic code. Whatever body we were meant to have, we will be given. And everything God makes is good.

155.
MY HUSBAND WORKS VERY HARD AS A PASTOR OF A SMALL CHURCH AND DOESN'T GET MUCH THANKS AND CERTAINLY NOT MUCH FINANCIAL REWARD. I KEEP REMINDING HIM THAT HE WILL BE REWARDED IN HEAVEN. CAN YOU TELL ME ABOUT THESE REWARDS?

Heavenly rewards are not limited to a chosen few but are given "to all those who have waited with love for him to come again" (2 Tim. 4:8 NCV). The three-letter word *all* is a gem. The winner's circle isn't reserved for a handful of the elite but is for a heaven full of God's children who "will receive the crown of life that God has promised to those who love him" (James 1:12).

For all we don't know about the next life, this much is certain. The day Christ comes will be a day of reward. Those who went unknown on earth will be known in heaven. Those who never heard the cheers of people will hear the cheers of angels. Those who missed the blessing of a father will hear the blessing of their heavenly Father.

The small will be great. The forgotten will be remembered. The unnoticed will be crowned, and the faithful will be honored. "Be faithful until death, and I will give you the crown of life" (Rev. 2:10 NKJV).

Your day is coming. What the world has overlooked, your Father has remembered, and sooner than you can imagine, you will be blessed by him. Look at this promise from the pen of Paul: "God will praise each one of them" (1 Cor. 4:5 NCV).

What an incredible sentence. God will praise each one of them. Not "the best of them" nor "a few of them" nor "the achievers among them," but "God will praise each one of them."

You won't be left out. God will see to that. In fact, God himself will give the praise. When it comes to giving recognition, God does not delegate the job. Michael doesn't hand out the crowns. Gabriel doesn't speak on behalf of the throne. God himself does the honors. God himself will praise his children.

While we're not sure exactly what those rewards are, we do know they include heavenly applause, God's approval, and eternal life. What else would you want?

156.
What does God think of suicide victims? What does that mean for their salvation? For our memories? For our peace of mind?

Suicide victims battled life's rawest contests. They often faced a mental illness or illnesses and felt the peril of mental fatigue. What you and I take for granted, they coveted. Optimism. Hope. Confidence that all will be well. Their clouds had no silver linings; their storms had no rainbows.

Didn't we wonder, *Why couldn't he snap out of this slump . . . shrug off this case of the blues . . . buck up and move forward?* Of course, had the struggle been a physical one, we wouldn't have asked those questions. Of cancer patients we don't ask, "Why didn't they get rid of that melanoma?" We understand the power of cancer. We may not understand the mystery of mental illness. I certainly don't. But this much I have observed. Depression causes good people to make the wrong choice.

Let's be clear: suicide is the wrong choice. The date of our death is God's to choose, not ours. He gives life, and he takes it. When people orchestrate their own death, they make the wrong choice.

But is the mistake a spiritually fatal one? Do we despair of any hope of their eternal salvation? Are we left with the nightmarish conclusion that heaven holds no place for them?

By no means. For while suicide is the wrong choice, have not we all made wrong choices? And did Christ not come for people like us? Frame their lives rightly. Remember good decisions. Catalog blue-ribbon days. Jesus said, "Come to Me, all you who labor and are heavy laden, and I will give you rest" (Matt. 11:28 NKJV). God does not measure a person by one decision, nor should we.

157.

WHAT WILL HAPPEN ON JUDGMENT DAY? WHEN CHRIST COMES BACK, WILL EVERYONE SEE HIM?

The Bible tantalizes us with the sights and sounds of that day. First, the shout. "For the Lord Himself will descend from heaven with a shout" (1 Thess. 4:16 NKJV).

Next, the resurrection of the bodies. "The dead will hear the voice of the Son of God . . . all who are . . . in their graves will hear his voice. Then they will come out" (John 5:25, 28–29 NCV).

The shout of God will trigger "the voice of an archangel, and . . . the trumpet of God" (1 Thess. 4:16 NKJV).

Angels everywhere! "The Lord is coming with thousands and thousands of holy angels to judge everyone" (Jude 14–15 CEV).

And people everywhere! "All the nations will be gathered before Him" (Matt. 25:32 NKJV).

At some point in this grand collection, our spirits will be reunited with our bodies. "It will happen in a moment, in the blink of an eye, when the last trumpet is blown. For when the trumpet sounds, those who have died will be raised to live forever. And we who are living will also be transformed. For our dying bodies must be transformed into bodies that will never die; our mortal bodies must be transformed into immortal bodies" (1 Cor. 15:52–53 NLT).

Noise will erupt around us. "On that day heaven will pass away with a roaring sound. Everything that makes up the universe will burn and be destroyed. The earth and everything that people have done on it will be exposed" (2 Peter 3:10 GOD'S WORD).

Then the highlight: "the Son of Man coming on the clouds of heaven with power and great glory" (Matt. 24:30 TEV). "Every knee will bow to the name of Jesus—everyone in heaven, on earth, and under the earth. And everyone will confess that Jesus Christ is Lord" (Phil. 2:10–11 NCV).

Stay ready. We do not know when he will come, but we know he will. May he find us watching.

158. Is it true that all our sins will be revealed at judgment? If so, I will melt in shame.

Jesus said, "There is nothing concealed that will not be disclosed, or hidden that will not be made known" (Matt. 10:26).

Those words would seem like a reason for panic. Who of us would like to have our secret thoughts made public? Who would want our private sins published? Who would get excited over the idea that every wrong deed we've ever done will be announced to everyone?

You're right; no one would.

Romans 2:16 is a key verse on this question. Let out a sigh of relief as you underline these three words: "This will take place on the day when God will judge men's secrets *through Jesus Christ*" (emphasis mine).

Did you see it? Jesus is the screen through which God looks when he judges our sins.

When God looks at those who have believed, he doesn't see them; he sees the One who surrounds them. That means that failure is not a concern for you. Your victory is secure.

159.
ONE OF MY HIGH SCHOOL FRIENDS BELIEVES IN PURGATORY. SHE LIGHTS CANDLES AND PRAYS THAT HER DEAD RELATIVES WILL GET TO HEAVEN. CAN WE PRAY FOR THE DEAD TO BE SAVED? DOES PURGATORY REALLY EXIST?

The idea that we all have a second chance, as we sit in the waiting room of spirits, to figure out our lives, to see where we've gone wrong, and to work out our problems gives some hope to the grieving. We firmly believe that once we cast off this body, lose our busy schedules, and have some time to think, we'll make the right choices.

Unfortunately, we find no support for that place in the Bible.

Jesus also never mentioned purgatory. He talked about only two places in the afterlife—heaven and hell. Nothing in between.

Purgatory is described as a place where we are purged or cleansed from our sins. Advocates claim that in purgatory people receive the punishment they deserve, suffer the consequences, then leave after a period of time—once they've learned their lesson—entering paradise prepared and renewed.

If that's the case, then what did Jesus do on the cross? Didn't he die and suffer for our sins? He didn't suffer for his own sins—I know that. Didn't his sacrifice offer 100 percent forgiveness to those who believe? Or was it only 70, 80, or 90 percent, and we have to make up the difference?

On that cross Jesus turned to his newest follower, the thief, and said, "Today you will be with me in paradise" (Luke 23:43) not, "Today I will see you in purgatory where you can suffer some more." The word *paradise* indicates no suffering. That's why we call it paradise.

Jesus also said, "It is finished," as he slipped away to death (John 19:30). Was there more to his statement? Did he mean to say, "It is finished . . . until you go to purgatory and finish the work that I have started," but got cut off?

"It is finished" means it is finished! No more needs to be done. Finis! Finito!

Romans 6:23 says the wages of sin is death. How could we withstand the punishment of death that we deserve? The punishment is death, and in purgatory people would already be dead.

Purgatory is suggested by some to be a hell with hope. What hope can we find in paying for our sins? How long would that take? Are we beat into submission until we accept Christ? Belief by coercion?

The good news is that Jesus already purged us of our sins. Calvary was our purgatory. As a believer steps out of his human costume and into his clean, heavenly robes, he does so with the assurance that Jesus Christ paid it all. Paradise, not purgatory, awaits.

160.
OUR SUNDAY SCHOOL CLASS HAD A DISCUSSION ABOUT HEAVEN THE OTHER DAY. SOME SAID THAT OUR PRIORITY THERE WILL BE TO PRAISE GOD. OTHERS SAID WE WILL BE WORKING FOR GOD. WHAT WILL WE BE DOING IN HEAVEN?

While praise and worship dominate the itinerary in heaven, does that mean we sing of God's love forever? Praise and worship do not always mean singing. In fact, we can praise and worship God by picking fruit and naming animals.

That's what Adam and Eve did. As soon as they rolled off the assembly line, God gave them garden duty. "Let them have dominion" (Gen. 1:26 NKJV). He gave them responsibility "over the fish of the sea, over the birds of the air, and over the cattle, over all the earth and over every creeping thing that creeps on the earth" (v. 26 NKJV). God made Adam the executive in charge of garden maintenance and growth (2:15).

So if God put us on earth to work, is heaven our retirement plan? An eternal cruise basking in the light of the Lord while angels serve us drinks?

God made people to serve, and that service does not end when we die. When we arise from the graves, in the new heaven and new earth, it will be our privilege to serve the Lord and others, using our God-given talents, while we explore our passions in heaven, on earth, and, who knows, maybe throughout the universe.

Maybe you'll serve him in the capacity you serve him now at church— teacher, hospitality, music, drama. Maybe your job in heaven will reflect your job on earth—designer, contractor, chef, decorator, engineer, concierge, entertainer. Maybe you'll finally discover that long-dormant, hidden passion you were unable to explore on earth so that you get to enjoy it in heaven.

God has expansion plans in the future. "Of the increase of His government and peace there will be no end" (Isa. 9:7 NKJV). Eternity is filled with increase— unexplored regions, expanding horizons, infinite colors, unending playlists. Maybe God keeps creating and we keep enjoying.

We were made to work, and we were made to worship. Put them together, and you have your eternal itinerary in heaven.

161.

OUR LOVELY TEENAGE DAUGHTER WAS KILLED IN A MOTORCYCLE ACCIDENT A FEW MONTHS AGO. WE KNOW SHE IS WITH JESUS, BUT WE WONDER WHAT SHE IS LIKE. WILL WE RECOGNIZE HER IN HEAVEN? OR WILL SHE BE DIFFERENT?

In heaven we will all be changed, in a twinkling of an eye. In that moment our bodies, upgraded for eternity, will reunite with our spirits.

In that spirit we find our heart, soul, and mind, the essence of what makes us who we are. Will we—you and I and your daughter—be exactly the same as we were on earth?

I hope not.

We will be better.

Gone from our personality will be the evil and filth. "Nothing that is impure will enter the city" (Rev. 21:27 TEV). All the sin that blackened our hearts will be washed clean. All the razor-sharp comments that filled our minds checked at the door.

Gone will be all the hurt that shaped our outlook on life, all the disease that kept us from hope.

What will emerge is a better, brighter, and purer child of God with decades of earthly waste stripped away. The personality that walks into heaven will be the one God always saw in us, the cleaned-up version that just needed a good heavenly bath.

You will be you at your best, forever!

And you'll enjoy all the other people in their prime! As it is, one of us is always a step behind. Bad moods infect the best of families. Complaints shadow the clearest days. Bad apples spoil bunches of us, but rotten fruit doesn't qualify for the produce section of heaven. Christ will have completed his redemptive work. All gossip excised and jealousy extracted. He will suction the last drop of orneriness from the most remote corners of our souls. You'll love the result. No one will doubt your word, question your motives, or speak evil behind your back. God's sin purging discontinues all strife.

In heaven you will certainly recognize your daughter, as sweet as she can be, sweeter than you can even imagine.

162.

MY PROBLEM IS THAT, ON THE ONE HAND, I'M GLAD I HAVE THE ASSURANCE I'LL GO TO HEAVEN. BUT ON THE OTHER HAND, I FEAR THAT I WON'T BE ME IN HEAVEN. HOW CAN I LOOK FORWARD TO HEAVEN WHEN I HAVE THIS FEAR OF THE UNKNOWN?

It has to be you in heaven for a number of reasons.

God saved you from your sins. Not your stunt double. Not your twin brother. Not some guy with the same Facebook name as you. But you.

It's you he fell in love with. Not some hologram or avatar of you in the future. Why would he want to hang around an impostor for eternity? He worked so hard to get your attention and develop a relationship with you on earth. God wants you with him forever.

If it's not you in heaven, why would you praise God? The itinerary of eternity is filled with devotion toward Jesus for saving us from our sins. If it's not you, then you don't know if God saved you. Since you don't know what you were saved from, you don't have any reason to praise God.

Without our identities in heaven, there would be no reunions. Spouses would become strangers. Our children would be foreigners. We would have an odd sense of déjà vu around this guy who thinks he was our neighbor. God is all about relationships and reconciliation on earth. Why would he change his tune in heaven?

In Luke 16, Jesus told a story about a rich man in hell. He pleads with Abraham to give him some relief. Abraham refuses. "But Abraham replied, 'Son, remember that in your lifetime you received your good things'" (v. 25). Abraham knew the rich man could remember his life.

The rich man tries another request. "He answered, 'Then I beg you, father, send Lazarus to my father's house, for I have five brothers. Let him warn them, so that they will not also come to this place of torment'" (vv. 27–28). The rich man, in his uncomfortable conscious state, knows he has relationships on earth—his father, his brothers. He does not suffer from eternal amnesia.

These rules of awareness in hell must also apply to heaven.

Revelation speaks of your name written in the Book of Life, the registry for eternal reservations.

> He who overcomes will, like them, be dressed in white. I will never blot out his name from the book of life, but will acknowledge his name before my Father and his angels. (Rev. 3:5)

When we pass through, we receive some identification labels, yet they don't change our identity.

> Him who overcomes I will make a pillar in the temple of my God. Never again
> will he leave it. I will write on him the name of my God and the name of the
> city of my God, the new Jerusalem, which is coming down out of heaven from
> my God; and I will also write on him my new name. (v. 12)

Like a box heading through shipping, marked with labels, we receive identification to move us along in processing. We are stamped with "God's Property," "Destined for Heaven," and "Belongs to Jesus."

While the stamps on us may be new, it's us on the inside—the same old person Jesus fell in love with before we were born—redeemed and made new in Christ.

163.

TO BE HONEST, HEAVEN DOES NOT EXCITE ME—THIS IDEA OF CLOUDS AND HARPS AND ENDLESS SINGING. WHAT AM I MISSING?

You're missing a big point about heaven. Forget the cherubs and disembodied spirits. Heaven will be this world at its best. God has not forgotten Eden. All of nature looks toward delivery. Safe within her womb is the soon-to-be-born cosmos. "The created world itself can hardly wait for what's coming next" (Rom. 8:19 MSG). God's material world won't disappear but will reappear in its perfect form.

Why would God abandon his planet? He never renounced his work. Quite the opposite. He pledged to restore it: "Behold, I will create new heavens and a new earth" (Isa. 65:17). The Greek language has two words for *new*. One suggests chronology; the other suggests quality. The English language offers the same options. The phrase "new kitchen" can mean "brand-new," as in one that never existed before. Or it can mean "new and improved" as in one with new appliances and fixtures. When John says, "I saw a new heaven and a new earth" (Rev. 21:1), which *new* do you suppose he employs?

He picks quality, not chronology. He sees, not an earth that has never been, but an earth that has not been so splendid since the days of Eden.

Why would God give you such love for his earth if he only intends to destroy it? The woodland glade. The breath-stealing oak. The stars that dance like dewdrops in the sky. Why does he give us a love for his creation? Because he tantalizes. He woos. He dangles a Yosemite waterfall or Caribbean coast in our direction and says, "This is just a sample of what awaits you. The best of this world is a postcard of the next." The earth is God's hors d'oeuvre tray.

Snowflakes in heaven? Giraffes and groundhogs? Misty glades and star-studded nights? Yes, this and much more. Let the glory of this life whet your appetite for the next. The universe is a pregnant creation. But she will give birth . . . and when she does, God will be one proud Father.

164. In family devotions the other night, my little girl asked whether in heaven we get our own room. I'm at a loss for an answer. What should I tell her?

> Don't let your hearts be troubled. Trust in God, and trust also in me. There is more than enough room in my Father's home. If this were not so, would I have told you that I am going to prepare a place for you? When everything is ready, I will come and get you, so that you will always be with me where I am. (John 14:1–3 NLT)

Jesus gives us the address to his home, and he invites us to the ultimate housewarming party in heaven. As a bonus, he even offers to build us a place to live and make room for us.

In Jewish times a person built a house or received the house from his father as an inheritance. As the family grew, the father added new rooms to his house to accommodate sons and their families—spouses and grandchildren. Maybe a sister fell on hard times. Well, they made room for her. There could even be a guest room for visitors passing through town.

At the center of the house was a courtyard, which served as the kitchen for the family dinners or as a place just to hang out and chat.

Jesus calls heaven the Father's house. It conveys a picture of a main room for the Father—a throne room perhaps—with little rooms built on the outskirts of a central meeting area. There we could hold worship rallies or dine on those big feasts Jesus promised us or just hang out for eternal quality time.

This is just a picture of the comfort and closeness we will feel with our Father in heaven. It will be more than a house. It will be a home.

Will we have our own separate rooms where we can disappear and chill? If God feels we need that, then, sure, we'll have that. Unfortunately, for many, rooms cause isolation and separation. That's not the theme of heaven. Heaven is about relationships, not walls.

But if the blueprints of heaven include private rooms, we will know it's exactly what God feels we need. Just tell your daughter to make sure she puts up a poster of Jesus on the wall and not a rock star.

165.
AN ARMY BUDDY OF MINE WAS KILLED BY AN EXPLOSIVE DEVICE. I HAD WITNESSED TO HIM, BUT HE NEVER WANTED ANYTHING TO DO WITH GOD. ON TOP OF MY GRIEF, I'M WORRIED THAT HE WILL BE IN HELL.

In Mark 4, Jesus told his apostles about four kinds of soil and their response to seeds. He compared those soils to hearts that receive the Word of God. Three of them, because they forget to nurture, protect, water, and pull out the thorny weeds, do not allow truth to blossom.

As for your situation, first of all, I think Jesus would thank you for witnessing to your friends. Even the unresponsive ones. Especially the does-this-make-any-difference friends. You showed tremendous courage by risking your relationship for the love of your friend and your Savior.

Also, please don't beat yourself up. Your job is to throw seeds. That's all. Those seeds land in all sorts of places. It's up to others—your friends—to accept or reject that kernel of truth.

I have found that people who say they want nothing to do with Christ sometimes do. Their outward defenses say no, but their inner heart says yes.

You have no idea how deeply those seeds took root and grew. It's not your job to know. Just to throw. Let God grow.

Finally, God will judge your friend based on how much he received, how much he understood, how much he rejected, and how much he accepted. It's the fairest judgment any of us will ever experience.

166.
A FRIEND OF MINE HAS DRIFTED AWAY FROM GOD. HE SAYS HE WAS RAISED TO BELIEVE THAT GOD CHOOSES WHO WILL BE SAVED, AND HE FIGURES GOD DIDN'T CHOOSE HIM. CAN YOU HELP ME UNDERSTAND THIS? DO WE CHOOSE GOD, OR DOES GOD CHOOSE US?

In Matthew 22, Jesus told the story of a wedding banquet a king held for his son. The guests of honor received an invitation to come, but on the big day no one showed up. The guests flat-out refused the opportunity. The king, naturally upset (hey, he is the king, and kings tend to throw huge parties), told the servants to take the invitations to the streets, inviting anyone who wanted to come. The response was huge. The wedding hall filled with guests who wanted to be there with the king and his son.

While the festivities rocked on, the king spotted one guy without the proper attire. He had snuck in! Intruder alert! The king got the bouncers and tossed him out, saying, "Many are invited, but few are chosen" (v. 14).

So who gets the invitation to spend eternity with God, our King, and Jesus, his Son? Those who first read the Scriptures got first crack at it. The Pharisees and religious leaders read the invitations clearly outlined in the Old Testament—the prophecies and promises. They saw it with their own eyes, yet they refused to come to Jesus' birthday party.

Then the servants—the apostles, disciples, evangelists, pastors—took the message to the streets of Jerusalem, Nazareth, Jericho, New York, Sao Paulo, Bangladesh, Nairobi, and Warsaw and invited anyone who wanted to come. For a couple thousand years, millions have accepted that invitation.

So who is doing the choosing—God or us?

In the parable the king chose to invite others. The inviters chose whom to invite. And the invitees chose whether to accept. Choosing happened on many levels.

"God so loved the world," John 3:16 says. Not "God so loved only certain people in the world." Everyone's invited. "The Lord is not slow in keeping his promise, as some understand slowness. He is patient with you, not wanting anyone to perish, but everyone to come to repentance" (2 Peter 3:9). God wants everyone to come to the eternal party.

However, that parable ends on an odd note. What's this "many are invited, but few are chosen" comment?

The door is open for anyone to come, yet some guests violate the "No shirt, no shoes, no service" policy. They try to get in, but their clothes are soiled, filthy from sin. The dress code for heaven requires pure righteousness, white as snow. It's God's policy. He chose it.

God chooses for all to come, yet in his omniscience he knows who will accept the invitation. Many will refuse. Many will accept. Some will try to sneak in, yet God chooses to enforce his Forgiven-Only policy—only those who have accepted Jesus as their Savior are allowed in.

167.

WHAT OF THE PEOPLE WHO NEVER HEARD OF GOD? HOW CAN GOD JUDGE THEM FOR WHAT THEY DO NOT KNOW?

Certainly there are millions. The Native American who never knew about Bethlehem or Calvary. The Bronze Age farmer who predated the apostle Paul. The emotionally disturbed adult or mentally handicapped child. What about babies? Will God punish those who die in infancy or childhood and never live long enough to comprehend God's grace?

No. He will not. Heaven's population includes throngs of people who learned the name of their Savior when they awoke in their eternal home. I believe this for several reasons. "The Lord is . . . not willing that any should perish but that all should come to repentance" (2 Peter 3:9 NKJV). His mercy is as wide as his world. His invitation list is as long as his creation list. Would God predestine a person to perdition by virtue of geography or genealogy?

God's degree of revelation differs from person to person. He does not send the gospel message to all individuals in the same manner, to the same extent, and with the same force. God gave the apostles eyewitness moments. Jesus let Thomas touch his wounds and Peter see his empty tomb (John 20:26–28; 20:1–7). He granted the apostle Paul a dramatic heavenly vision (2 Cor. 12:1–4). He gave Max Lucado access to the Bible, godly parents, and the great influence of godly friends. I did not receive what Paul did, but I did receive what I needed to make my choice.

Would anyone receive any less? The citizen of Mongolia and the autistic child—will they receive anything less than what they need to put their faith in God? How could the answer be anything other than no? God, who loves all, will give all—all they need to make a decision for or against him.

At a minimum they have the testimony of creation and conscience. "They know the truth about God because he has made it obvious to them. For ever since the world was created, people have seen the earth and sky. Through everything God made, they can clearly see his invisible qualities—his eternal power and divine nature. So they have no excuse for not knowing God" (Rom. 1:19–20 NLT).

The cosmos around us. The convictions within us. What we see and what we sense convey the essence of God's character to every person. If this is all a person has, it is all the person needs. Is it possible, then, that some saved saints will learn the name of their Savior in heaven? Absolutely. The Bible teaches that heaven has residents "from every nation and tribe and people and language" (Rev. 7:9 NLT).

Every people group and tongue is represented. This must include people who responded, in faith, to a Savior they had yet to meet. Hebrews 9:15 explains that "Christ died so that the people who lived under the first agreement could be set free from sin" (NCV). Jesus' grace stretches from the cross in all directions.

168.

I DON'T LIKE THE NARROW-MINDEDNESS OF CHRISTIANS. IT IS ABSURD TO SAY THAT JESUS IS THE ONLY WAY TO HEAVEN.

We need to accept one another. I agree. We need to be civil, respectful, and kind. But we don't need to gloss over our differences. Christianity is different from other religions.

Every non-Christian religion says, "You can save you." Jesus says, "My death on the cross saves you" (see John 10:9).

How can all religions lead to God when they are so different? We don't tolerate such illogic in other matters. We don't pretend that all roads lead to London or all ships sail to Australia. All flights don't land in Rome. Imagine your response to a travel agent who claims they do. You tell him you need a flight to Rome, Italy, so he looks at his screen.

"Well, there is a flight to Sydney, Australia, departing at 6:00 a.m."

"Does it go to Rome?"

"No, but it offers wonderful in-flight dining and movies."

"But I need to go to Rome."

"Then let me suggest Southwest Airlines."

"Southwest Airlines flies to Rome?"

"No, but they have consistently won awards for on-time arrivals."

You're growing frustrated. "I need one airline to carry me to one place: Rome."

The agent appears offended. "Sir, all flights go to Rome."

You know better. Different flights have different destinations. That's not a thickheaded conclusion but an honest one. Every flight does not go to Rome. Every path does not lead to God. The religions of the world are inherently different.

- ~ Judaism denies the New Testament and sees salvation as a Judgment Day decision based on morality. The Messiah, they believe, will bring peace to Israel . . . someday.
- ~ Hindus anticipate multiple reincarnations in the soul's journey through the cosmos. They believe in many gods, all of them impersonal.
- ~ Buddhism grades your life according to the Four Noble Truths and the Noble Eightfold Path. Heaven is nirvana, and it's all yours after multiple reincarnations.
- ~ Muslims earn their way to Allah by performing the duties of the Five Pillars of Faith. They say Jesus was not crucified, deny the Trinity, and raise Muhammad higher than any other prophet.

By contrast, Jesus blazed a stand-alone trail void of self-salvation. He cleared a one-of-a-kind passageway uncluttered by human effort. Christ came, not for the strong, but for the weak; not for the righteous, but for the sinner. We enter his way upon confession of our need, not completion of our deeds. He offers a unique-to-him invitation in which he works and we trust, he dies and we live, he invites and we believe.

169.

New Testament language leads some godly scholars to believe hell has a final date.

> Fear Him who is able to destroy both soul and body in hell. (Matt. 10:28 NKJV)

> Whoever believes in him shall not perish. (John 3:16)

Destroy. Perish. Don't such words imply an end to suffering? I wish I could say they do. There is no point on which I'd more gladly be wrong than the eternal duration of hell. If God, on the Last Day, extinguishes the wicked, I'll celebrate my misreading of his words. Yet annihilation seems inconsistent with Scripture. God sobers his warnings with eternal language. Consider John's description of the wicked in Revelation 14:11: "the smoke of their torment goes up forever and ever, and they have no rest, day or night" (ESV). How could the euthanized soul "have no rest, day or night"?

Jesus paralleled hell with gehenna, a rubbish dump outside the southwestern walls of Jerusalem, infamous for its unending smoldering and decay. He employs *gehenna* as a word picture of hell, the place where the "worm does not die and the fire is not quenched" (Mark 9:48 ESV). A deathless worm and a quenchless fire—however symbolic these phrases may be—smack of ongoing consumption of something. Jesus spoke of sinners being "thrown outside, into the darkness, where there will be weeping and gnashing of teeth" (Matt. 8:12). How can a nonexistent person weep or gnash teeth?

Jesus described the length of heaven and hell with the same adjective: *eternal.* "They will go away into eternal punishment, but the righteous into eternal life" (Matt. 25:46 RSV). Hell lasts as long as heaven.

Much perishes in hell. Hope perishes. Happiness perishes. But the body and soul of the God-deniers dwell forever there.

170.

I'VE BEEN TALKING TO A FRIEND IN SCHOOL, AND HE SEEMS VERY INTERESTED IN LEARNING ABOUT GOD AND SALVATION, BUT HE KEEPS COMING BACK TO ONE QUESTION: "HOW COULD A LOVING GOD SEND PEOPLE TO HELL?" CAN YOU HELP ME ANSWER THIS QUESTION?

First, God does not *send* people to hell. He simply honors their choice. Hell is the ultimate expression of God's high regard for the dignity of humans. He has never forced us to choose him, even when that means we would choose hell instead. As C. S. Lewis stated, "There are only two kinds of people in the end: those who say to God, 'Thy will be done,' and those to whom God says, in the end, '*Thy* will be done.' All that are in Hell, choose it."[2] In another book Lewis said it this way: "I willingly believe that the damned are, in one sense, successful, rebels to the end; that the doors of hell are locked on the *inside*."[3]

No, God does not "send" people to hell. Nor does he send "people" to hell.

The word *people* is neutral, implying innocence. Nowhere does Scripture teach that innocent people are condemned. People do not go to hell. Sinners do. The rebellious do. The self-centered do. So how could a loving God send people to hell? He doesn't. He simply honors the choice of sinners. Hell declares God's justice.

If there is no hell, God is not just. If there is no punishment of sin, heaven is apathetic toward the rapists and pillagers and mass murderers of society. If there is no hell, God is blind toward the victims and has turned his back on those who pray for relief. If there is no wrath toward evil, then God is not love, for love hates that which is evil. As much as we resist the idea, isn't the absence of hell even worse?

In the end, God saves those who want to be saved and dismisses those who don't.

171. Exactly where is hell? Is it in the center of the earth? Out in space? Where does it exist?

Hell exists in the same realm as heaven. Right now it's a spiritual address, where no earthly mailman can deliver, no astronaut can dock, and no oil-well digger can drill. Just as you can't climb a ladder and rest its end on a cumulus nimbus to drop in and see Moses, you can't take a swan dive into the cavern and expect to land on a demon's back.

Jesus gave one chilling clue about hell's address: it's outside. "Tie him hand and foot, and throw him outside, into the darkness" (Matt. 22:13).

Outside of what? Outside the boundaries of heaven, for one thing.

Abraham, in paradise, told the rich man, in torment, "Between us and you there is a great gulf fixed, so that those who want to pass from here to you cannot, nor can those from there pass to us" (Luke 16:26 NKJV).

Hell is outside God's will. God desires all to know him and accept his Son. Those who dwell in hell moved away from God's will and into their own desired acceptance of themselves as a means of salvation.

Hell is outside God's love. God sends out Valentine's Day cards every day, every moment to people, announcing his love for them. They are returned to sender. Rejected. They prefer the love of the world.

Hell is outside eternal productivity. In hell, all the world's dreams, accomplishments, awards, hopes, and monuments burn up. No one takes their medals with them. All of them go into the trash. Only eternal things enter eternity. You, me, and the souls we brought with us.

Hell is outside God's blessing. Wherever God lives, so do hope and happiness, laughter and encouragement. He's the life of the party. Wherever he isn't, the mood is somber.

Hell is outside God's illumination. The most common description of hell is darkness. No one there can see clearly, stumbling over themselves and their sins.

While hell is a spiritual place right now, there will come a time when it becomes real and tangible. Revelation 20:14 tells us that after the resurrection, death and the grave will be thrown into the lake of fire. This is the second death. The first death is a person's death on earth, separating him from his body. The second death unites the soul and an eternal body but separates the person eternally, forever, from God and the new heaven and new earth.

Hell is about separation, being outside of God.

I know . . . it is a dreadful, dreadful thought.

172.

WITH THE CURRENT TURMOIL IN THE WORLD, MY FRIEND SAYS HE'S SURE JESUS IS COMING SOON. SO HE HAS QUIT HIS JOB AND SPENDS HIS DAYS PRAYING AND WAITING FOR JESUS TO COME BACK. IT SOUNDS NOBLE BUT ALSO A BIT CRAZY. IS THIS THE RIGHT THING TO DO?

Absolutely not. Jesus' imminent return does not give us permission to give up but is an invitation to get busy. There's *work* to be done, because when Jesus returns, that's it. The final finale. The tolling of the bell.

While we work, we must *wait*. Paul says, "We are hoping for something we do not have yet, and we are waiting for it patiently" (Rom. 8:25 NCV). Simeon is our model. While waiting for the Messiah, he was not so consumed with the "not yet" that he ignored the "right now" (Luke 2:25–35). Luke says Simeon was a "good man and godly" (v. 25 NCV). Our job is waiting, yet we work with anticipation and expectation.

While we wait, we must *watch*. "The day of the Lord will come like a thief. The skies will disappear with a loud noise. Everything in them will be destroyed by fire, and the earth and everything in it will be burned up. In that way everything will be destroyed. So what kind of people should you be?" (2 Peter 3:10–11 NCV).

Great question, Peter. What kind of people should we be?

While we watch, we must be *witnesses*. Peter tells us: "You should live holy lives and serve God, as you wait for and look forward to the coming of the day of God" (vv. 11–12 NCV).

Hope in the future is not a license for irresponsibility in the present. We must not become so patient that we become complacent or too content.

It is to those of us who are strong in waiting and weak in watching that our Lord was speaking when he said, "No one knows when that day or time will be, not the angels in heaven, not even the Son. Only the Father knows . . . So always be ready, because you don't know the day your Lord will come . . . The Son of Man will come at a time you don't expect him" (Matt. 24:36, 42, 44 NCV).

Simeon reminds us to wait forwardly. Patiently vigilant. Not so patient that we lose our vigilance. Nor so vigilant that we lose our patience.

Addendum

The Write Stuff

In our office we receive many questions about writing: how to write, when to write, who can publish, who can edit. Not a week passes that we don't receive a question about writing. So I wrote down a few thoughts. Hope you find them helpful.[1]

We like to envision him as an old man with young eyes, wild hair, and a raging quill. He wrote by the light of a lamp in the lee of a shack with the fury of a prophet. His pen could scarcely keep pace with his thoughts.

> A revealing of Jesus, the Messiah. God gave it to make plain to his servants what is about to happen. He published and delivered it by Angel to his servant John. And John told everything he saw: God's Word—the witness of Jesus Christ!
>
> How blessed the reader! How blessed the hearers and keepers of these oracle words, all the words written in this book! (Rev. 1:1–3 MSG)

The old apostle paused only to catch his breath and dip his pen. He stood only to gaze through an open window into the just-opened heavens. If he closed his eyes, it was only to rummage through his treasure chest of words for the one that fit the vision of an often-crowned Christ or a blood-dipped robe. No lazy verbs, no vanilla adjectives. This gate glistened with pearls, and streets spoke of gold. This was God's revelation. John was God's revealer. So John wrote.

So did Paul. Yet Paul wrote, not because of heavenly action, but because of congregational angst. Titus needed direction; the Ephesians needed assurance. Timothy struggled, the Corinthians squabbled, and the Galatians waffled. So Paul wrote them.

How he made music with his words. He turned epistles into concert hall sheet music. "Though I speak with the tongues of men and of angels, but have not love, I have become sounding brass or a clanging cymbal" (1 Cor. 13:1 NKJV). It's as if he dipped his pen in honey. He could sound like a poet in the seventh heaven.

He could also sound like a pastor on Monday morning. Tired, frustrated. Beginning sentences and not finishing them. Starting a second thought before he completed the first. Throwing out ideas in lumps instead of lyrics. But that was okay. He wasn't writing the Bible. He was writing to Philemon. He wasn't crafting epistles; he was solving problems. Paul didn't write for the ages; he wrote for the churches. He wrote for souls.

So did Luke. Remember the early words of his gospel?

Since I have investigated all the reports in close detail, starting from the story's beginning, I decided to write it all out for you, most honorable Theophilus, so you can know beyond the shadow of a doubt the reliability of what you were taught. (Luke 1:3–4 MSG)

We wonder who Theophilus was and where Theophilus lived and if Theophilus found it unusual to receive a two-volume letter. We wonder what convinced Luke to rivet himself to his wooden chair near a shuttered window long enough to write a gospel. What prompted Dr. Luke to exchange his scalpel for the pen, the crowds for the quiet corner? When did he perceive his assignment as a kingdom scribe?

We wonder because we've wondered if God would use us to do the same.

We know a Theophilus or two. We've seen the confusion in Ephesus and heard of the troubles in Crete. And we've felt the sands of Patmos beneath our feet, its fire within our hearts. And we've written: articles, blogs, books, stories. Not like Luke, Paul, and John. But not unlike them either.

We've had our moments of inspiration. Sandwiched between hours of per-spiration, for sure. But we've had our moments—mystical moments of pounding heart and pounding keyboard. We've felt the wind at our backs and sensed a holy hand guiding ours. We, as our Creator, have beheld our creations and declared, "It's good." (Or at least, "It's not so bad.") And we have asked: Is this our call? Our assignment? To use words to shape souls?

I first ventured such a question beneath the balmy skies of Miami, Florida. I was a rookie minister in 1979. The church where I served published a weekly bulletin. Many pastors dread such assignments, but I came to cherish it. Tuesday evenings became my notebook date night. I would retreat with pad and pen and sit until something happened. Once a week I went into labor and delivered an idea. Is there any sweeter moment than the writing of the final sentence?

Actually there is. The appreciation thereof. When eighty-year-old Edith Hayes thanked me in the church foyer for my article on prayer. When Joe the boat builder gave copies to his crew. When the pastor from California urged me to write for publication. I smiled for days. It's one thing to write. It's quite another to be read.

I came to believe this much: good words are worth the work. Well-written words can change a life. Words go where we never go. Africa. Australia. Indonesia. My daughter was in Bangalore, India, last summer and saw my books in the display window of a shop.

Written words go to places you'll never go.

. . . and descend to depths you'll never know.

The readers invite the author to a private moment. They clear the calendar, find a corner, flip on the lamp, turn off the television, pour the tea, pull on the wrap, silence the dog, shoo the kids. They set the table, pull out the chair, and invite you, "Come, talk to me for a moment."

So accept the invitation. We need your writing. Pick up the pens left by Paul, John, and Luke, and write for the souls. They show us how.

For example, they always delivered the bread. Have you noticed?

They wrote with their lives first. They lived the message before they scribed it. John was under fire for his faith. ". . . was in the isle that is called Patmos" (Rev. 1:9 KJV). Exiled for his passion. Rome locked him up because they couldn't shut him up. And Paul? He did his writing and thinking about God in the middle and muddle of the world. On a boat crossing the sea or in a prison cell chained to a guard. Luke, it seems, had two loves, Jesus and Theophilus. And he wrote fifty-two chapters in hopes that the latter would meet the former.

They didn't inhabit ivory towers or quarantine themselves in a world of unasked questions. "You know . . . in what manner I always lived among you," Paul said (Acts 20:18 NKJV). Before he wrote about Christ, he lived Christ. He responded to a real world with real words. Let's do the same.

Let your life be your first draft. Shouldn't Christian writers be *Christian* writers? Love grumpy neighbors. Feed hungry people. Help a struggling church. Pay your bills, your dues, and attention to your spouse. You'll never write better than you live. Live with integrity.

And when it's time to write, write with clarity.

Good writing reflects clear thinking. Here's a tip:

Cherish clarity. Make it your aim to summarize the entire book in one sentence. Distill the message into a phrase, and protect it. Stand guard. Defy interlopers. No paragraph gets to play unless it contributes to the message of the book.

Follow the example of John.

Jesus worked many other miracles for his disciples, and not all of them are written in this book. But these are written so that you will put your faith in Jesus. (John 20:30–31 cev)

John self-edited. He auditioned his stories to fit the manuscript. He littered his floor with edited paragraphs.

Good writers do this. They tap the Delete button and distill the writing. They bare-bones and bare-knuckle it. They cut the fat and keep the fact. Concise (but not cute). Clear (but not shallow). Enough (but not too much).

Make every word earn its place on the page. Not just once or twice, but many times. Sentences can be like just-caught fish—spunky today and stinky tomorrow. Reread until you've thrown out all the stinkers. Rewrite until you have either a masterpiece or an angry publisher. Revise as long as you can. "God's words are pure words, pure silver words refined seven times in the fires of his word-kiln" (Psalm 12:6 msg).

Ernest Hemingway espoused rewriting: "I rise at first light . . . and I start by rereading and editing everything I have written to the point I left off. That way I go through a book I'm writing several hundred times . . . Most writers slough off the toughest but most important part of their trade—editing their stuff, honing it and honing it until it gets an edge like the bullfighter's *estoque*, the killing sword." Describing *A Farewell to Arms*, Hemingway said, "I had rewritten the ending thirty-nine times in manuscript and . . . worked it over thirty times in proof, trying to get it right."[2]

I find it helps to read the work out loud. First to myself, then to anyone who is kind enough to listen. I vary the locations of the reading. What sounds good in the study must sound good on the porch. What sounds good to me must sound good to my editors. Sure, editing hurts. So does a trip to the dentist. But someone needs to find the cavities.

Let editors do their job. Release your grip on the manuscript. A little red ink won't hurt you. A lot of red ink might save you. My most recent manuscript was returned to me sunburned in red. It bled like raw steak. Of its fourteen chapters, thirteen needed an overhaul. I was depressed for a week. Yet the book is better because of the editors.

And isn't that our aim? The best book possible? We need good books. We need your best book. The single ... the lonely pastor ... the stressed missionary—we need you to give them your best words. We need you to write.

Intending to write is not writing. Researching is not writing. Telling people you want to write is not writing. Writing is writing. Peter De Vries said, "I write when I'm inspired, and I see to it that I'm inspired at nine o'clock every morning."[3]

A framed quote greets me each time I sit at my desk. "You wanna write? Put your butt in that chair and sit there a long, long time." Writing is not glamorous work.

But it is a noble work. A valued work. A worthwhile work. A holy work. "How many a man," asked Thoreau, "has dated a new era in his life from the reading of a book!"[4]

May you write such books, give birth to new eras. May you see the heavens like John, love the churches like Paul, and touch the souls like Luke. May you pick up their pens and write for the soul.

Notes

Hope: God, Grace, and "Why am I here?"

1. A day's wage.
2. J. A. Motyer, *The Message of Philippians: Jesus Our Joy* (Downers Grove, IL: Inter-Varsity Press, 1984), 166.
3. Ronald J. Sider, *Rich Christians in an Age of Hunger: Moving from Affluence to Generosity* (Nashville: Thomas Nelson, 2005), 10.
4. Ibid., 35.
5. UNICEF, *The State of the World's Children 2009: Maternal and Newborn Health*, 133, www.unicef.org/sowc09/report/report.php.
6. The percentage of Christians in the United States is 76.8 percent, and the population of the United States in 2009 was approximately 307,212,000, according to the CIA, *The World Factbook*, 2009, www.cia.gov/library/publications/the-world-factbook/geos/us.html.
7. United Nations World Food Programme, *WFP Facts Blast, December 2009*, http://home.wfp.org/stellent/groups/public/documents/communications/wfp187701.pdf.
8. Anup Shah, "Today, Over 25,000 Children Died Around the World," *Global Issues*, www.globalissues.org/article/715/today-over-25000-children-died-around-the-world.

Hurt: Conflicts, Calamities, and "Why me?"

1. C. S. Lewis, *Mere Christianity* (New York: Macmillan, 1960), 106–7.
2. M. Paul Lewis, ed., *Ethnologue: Languages of the World*, 16th ed. (Dallas: SIL International, 2009), www.ethnologue.com.

Help: Prayer, Scripture, and "Why church?"

1. Brother Lawrence, *The Practice of the Presence of God* (Old Tappan, NJ: Revell, 1958), 9.
2. "U.S. & World Population Clocks," U.S. Census Bureau, www.census.gov/main/www/popclock.html (accessed July 28, 2010).

Him/Her: Sex, Romance, and "Any chance of a second chance?"

1. "Gender Differences in Our Approach to Sex," Marriage Missions International, www.marriagemissions.com/gender-differences-in-our-approach-to-sex.
2. David F. Greenberg, *The Construction of Homosexuality* (Chicago: University of Chicago Press, 1988), 195.

Haves/Have-Nots: Work, Money, and "Where's the lifeline?"

1. Bob Russell with Rusty Russell, *Money: A User's Manual* (Sisters, OR: Multnomah, 1997), 82.
2. Linda Kulman, "Our Consuming Interest," *U.S. News & World Report*, June 28–July 5, 2004, 59.

Hereafter: Cemeteries, Heaven, Hell, and "Who goes where?"

1. Ann Kaiser Stearns, *Living Through Personal Crisis* (1984; repr., Enumclaw, WA: Idyll Arbor, Inc., 2010), 6.
2. C. S. Lewis, *The Great Divorce* (New York: Macmillan, 1946), 72.
3. C. S. Lewis, *The Problem of Pain* (New York: HarperCollins, 2001), 130.

Addendum: The Write Stuff

1. "The Write Stuff" was originally presented at Jerry Jenkins's Christian Writers Guild Conference, Denver, CO, February 18, 2010.
2. A. E. Hotchner, *Papa Hemingway: A Personal Memoir* (Cambridge, MA: Da Capo Press, 2005), 114, 43.
3. Peter De Vries, ThinkExist.com, http://thinkexist.com/quotation/i_write_when_i-m_inspired-and_i_see_to_it_that_i/186988.html.
4. Henry David Thoreau, *Walden* (Nashville: American Renaissance, 2009), 56.

Topical Index

Scripture Index

The Lucado Reader's Guide

Discover . . . Inside every book by Max Lucado, you'll find words of encouragement and inspiration that will draw you into a deeper experience with Jesus and treasures for your walk with God. What will you discover?

3:16: The Numbers of Hope
… the 26 words that can change your life.
core scripture: John 3:16

And the Angels Were Silent
… what Jesus Christ's final days can teach you about what matters most.
core scripture: Matthew 20–27

The Applause of Heaven
… the secret to a truly satisfying life.
core scripture: The Beatitudes, Matthew 5:1–10

Come Thirsty
… how to rehydrate your heart and sink into the wellspring of God's love.
core scripture: John 7:37–38

Cure for the Common Life
… the unique things God designed you to do with your life.
core scripture: 1 Corinthians 12:7

Every Day Deserves a Chance
… how living in a purposeful way will help you trust more, stress less.
core scripture: Psalm 118:24

Facing Your Giants
… when God is for you, no challenge is too great.
core scripture: 1 and 2 Samuel

Fearless
… how faith is the antidote to the fear in your life.
core scripture: John 14:1,3

A Gentle Thunder
… the God who will do whatever it takes to lead his children back to Him.
core scripture: Psalm 81:7

The Great House of God
a blueprint for peace, joy, and love found in the Lord's Prayer.
core scripture: The Lord's Prayer, Matthew 6:9–13

God Came Near
… a love so great that it left heaven to become part of your world.
core scripture: John.1:14

He Chose the Nails
… a love so deep that it chose death on a cross—just to win your heart.
core scripture: 1 Peter 1:18–20

He Still Moves Stones
… the God who still does the impossible—in your life.
core scripture: Matthew 12:20

In the Eye of the Storm
… peace in the storms of your life.
core scripture: John 6

In the Grip of Grace
… the greatest gift of all—the grace of God.
core scripture: Romans

It's Not About Me
… why focusing on God will make sense of your life.
core scripture: 2 Corinthians 3:18

Just Like Jesus
… a life free from guilt, fear, and anxiety.
core scripture: Ephesians 4:23–24

A Love Worth Giving
… how living loved frees you to love others.
core scripture: 1 Corinthians 13

Next Door Savior
… a God who walked life's hardest trials—and still walks with you through yours.
core scripture: Matthew 16:13–16

No Wonder They Call Him the Savior
… hope in the unlikeliest place— upon the cross.
core scripture: Romans 5:15

Outlive Your Life
… that a great God created you to do great things.
core scripture: Acts 1

Six Hours One Friday
… forgiveness and healing in the middle of loss and failure.
core scripture: John 19–20

Traveling Light
… the power to release the burdens you were never meant to carry.
core scripture: Psalm 23

When God Whispers Your Name
… the path to hope in knowing that God knows you, never forgets you, and cares about the details of your life.
core scripture: John 10:3

When Christ Comes
… why the best is yet to come.
core scripture: 1 Corinthians 15:23

Recommended reading if you're struggling with . . .

FEAR AND WORRY

Come Thirsty
Fearless
For the Tough Times
Next Door Savior
Traveling Light

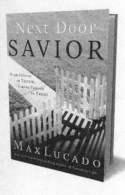

DISCOURAGEMENT

He Still Moves Stones
Next Door Savior

GRIEF/DEATH OF A LOVED ONE

Next Door Savior
Traveling Light
When Christ Comes
When God Whispers Your Name

GUILT

In the Grip of Grace
Just Like Jesus

LONELINESS

God Came Near

SIN

Facing Your Giants
He Chose the Nails
Six Hours One Friday

WEARINESS

When Got Whispers Your Name

Recommended reading if you want to know more about . . .

THE CROSS

And the Angels Were Silent
He Chose the Nails
No Wonder They Call Him the Savior
Six Hours One Friday

GRACE

He Chose the Nails
In the Grip of Grace

HEAVEN

The Applause of Heaven
When Christ Comes

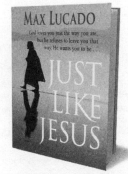

SHARING THE GOSPEL

God Came Near
No Wonder They Call Him the Savior

Recommended reading if you're looking for more . . .

COMFORT

For the Tough Times
He Chose the Nails
Next Door Savior
Traveling Light

COMPASSION

Outlive Your Life

COURAGE

Facing Your Giants
Fearless

HOPE

3:16: The Numbers of Hope
Facing Your Giants
A Gentle Thunder
God Came Near

JOY

The Applause of Heaven
Cure for the Common Life
When God Whispers Your Name

LOVE

Come Thirsty
A Love Worth Giving
No Wonder They Call Him the Savior

PEACE

And the Angels Were Silent
The Great House of God
In the Eye of the Storm
Traveling Light

SATISFACTION

And the Angels Were Silent
Come Thirsty
Cure for the Common Life
Every Day Deserves a Chance

TRUST

A Gentle Thunder
It's Not About Me
Next Door Savior

Max Lucado books make great gifts!

If you're coming up to a special occasion, consider one of these.

FOR ADULTS:

For the Tough Times
Grace for the Moment
Live Loved
The Lucado Life Lessons Study Bible
Mocha with Max
DaySpring Daybrighteners® and cards

FOR TEENS/GRADUATES:

Let the Journey Begin
You Can Be Everything God Wants You to Be
You Were Made to Make a Difference

FOR KIDS:

Just in Case You Ever Wonder
The Oak Inside the Acorn
You Are Special

FOR PASTORS AND TEACHERS:

God Thinks You're Wonderful
You Changed My Life

AT CHRISTMAS:

The Crippled Lamb
Christmas Stories from Max Lucado
God Came Near

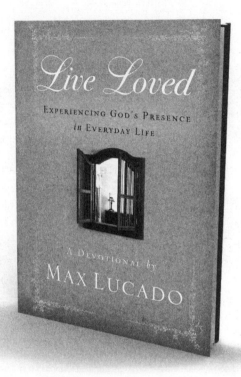

Address your biggest questions
about life and faith with guidance
from Max Lucado

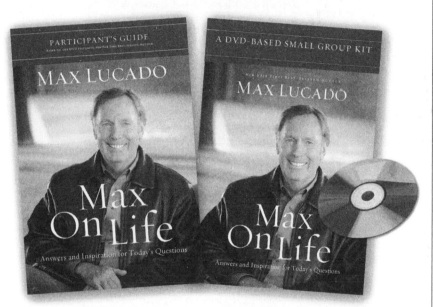

Max on Life Participants Guide
ISBN: 978-1-4185-4755-4 ($9.99)

Max on Life DVD-Based Small Group Kit
ISBN: 978-1-4185-4753-0 ($39.99)

The *Max on Life* DVD-Based Small Group Kit features four 12-to-15-minute video sessions featuring real-life stories of people who have faced the situations that give birth to some of our biggest questions about life and faith. From the profound (the role of prayer, the purpose of pain, the reason for our ultimate hope) to the day-to-day (parenting quandaries, financial challenges, difficult relationships), *Max on Life* is the perfect individual or small group study for both new and mature believers.

➤ Kit includes: DVD, 1 leader's guide, 1 participant's guide, & materials for promoting your group study, sermon series, or churchwide program.